A Childhood Tragedy Under A Mother's Watch

Part One: 1975-1982 Lowell Massachusetts

Catherine Mellen

NFB Publishing
Buffalo, New York

Copyright © 2021 Catherine Mellen
Printed in the United States of America
A Childhood Tragedy Under a Mother's Watch, Part One: 1975-1982 Lowell Massachusetts/Mellen- 1st Edition

ISBN: 978-1-953610-16-4

1.Title. 2. Memoir/Autobiography. 3. Childhood Trauma/Abuse. 4. Survivor. 5. Nonfiction.

No part of this book may be reproduced or transmitted in any form by any means, electronic or mechanical, including photocopying, recording, or by any information storage and retrieval system without permission in writing by the author.

NFB
<<<>>>
NFB Publishing/Amelia Press
119 Dorchester Road
Buffalo, New York 14213

For more information visit
Nfbpublishing.com

Dedicated to the children and adults who have unwilling become a statistic in a world full of abused children. May our strength be heard so no one dies a secret anymore.

Trigger Warning

Due to graphic detail of child rape and torture, please read with caution.

If you suffer from child rape or suspect a child is being abused, please call 1-800-387-5437 to report a concern to a Child Intervention caseworker. They are available in multiple languages, 24 hours a day.

Contents

Introduction	11
Shatter My Silence 1975-1977	15
A House of Horrors 1977-1981	32
A Family She Never Had 1981-1982	152
From the Author	182
Thank You {Poem}	187
About the Author	189

Introduction

Growing up I was often told by friends that their parents recognized me by my name as a child they had taken care of, or as the baby from the winter of 1969 when a mother was taken into protective custody by the Lowell police after she tried delivering me into a toilet in the bathroom stall of a local bar. The bar resided alongside Lowell's department of public works which made its home on the corners of Broadway and Fletcher Streets in the late 1960s and 1970s. I would hear so many stories about my mother and so many she told me herself. Like the story she told me of her own mother who had died when she was young. Leaving my mother to raise herself and then left to raise her kids all by herself also. Though I felt bad for the hard life my mother lived, I didn't think it was a good enough reason for how she treated me or allowed me to be treated. Of all the stories she had to share, she could never tell me what time I was born, how much I weighed or who I lived with when I was first born. Though I do not know the first years of my life, what I do know is…

I was born December 15, 1969 in Lowell, Massachusetts. The third daughter and seventh child to a woman whose lies would last as long as the number of children she would claim to have had. She met my father in the late 1960s. Their romance was a whirlwind that resulted in a marriage, pregnancy and a break-up of the marriage in just under two years. By the time I was born, their friendship was over.

YEARS had gone by when my aunt and uncle told me to get my doll from my room. They were upset while they held my hand as we got into their car for a ride. We stopped at a big house where my uncle held my hand as we walked into the building. We then walked down a small hallway and waited for a door to open. A woman answered the door and I walked into a room full of people. As I turned to my uncle, he motioned with his finger to his eye, his coat then to me. As I was about to ask him, "What?" the door slammed shut.

There were a lot of people in the house and soon I found myself remembering a dad I was told had died and wondering why my mother was a complete stranger to me as I adjusted myself on the couch next to a woman, I wasn't too sure of. We lived in a multi-unit building located diagonally across the North Common Park. A building formerly known as 346 Fletcher Street.

A true story of horrific abuse, cruelty, abandonment and one girl's fight to survive. An in-depth, graphic detailed look into childhood sexual abuse and family secrets.

Written by the child who survived it.

One
Shatter My Silence

346 Fletcher Street was a large multi apartment building which rested on the corner of Fletcher and Cross Street in the acre section of Lowell, Massachusetts. As you walked into the huge front door on the Fletcher Street side, immediately to your right was an apartment, straight ahead were stairs leading to more apartments and looking to the left side of those stairs was a little hall leading to the front door of a three-bedroom apartment. That is where I lived. As you opened the front door to the apartment, you walked into the kitchen, immediately to your right on the same wall was the doorway to the bathroom which had one of those old fashion porcelain tubs that rested on four legs above the floor. Directly to the left was the doorway to the living room and through that room was the bedroom my two brothers shared.

Back at the door, looking straight ahead was the large kitchen stove with the silver tube vent going into the wall and on the other side of the stove was the doorway to my bedroom. It had two twin beds along with a lot of other girl's clothes and toy's which now belonged to me. Back in the kitchen, if you go diagonally towards the right, there was a hallway where the snack cabinet was, a door going out to the backyard and the doorway to my mother's bedroom.

Exploring the neighborhood would keep the day busy as I played at local parks and the huge sand piles as unsupervised kids. I had a lot of freedom for a five-year-old kid. I lived with my two older brothers and my mother. The house was always full of strangers and the babysitters came and went. Some would stay for days while one took us to her home after my mother failed to show up for a few days. My mother wasn't much of a loving mother and always acted as if her children were an inconvenience to her. I would often get yelled at, smacked or sent to my room if I questioned her about my dad. I was told repeatedly my dad had died and that he never loved me. Every new boyfriend was another lecture of why I should call them, "Dad." Every break-up meant being pulled out of bed at all hours of the night so we could walk to local bars and watch my mother cause fights. Some days we were sent outside to play and were not allowed back inside until the door was unlocked.

My two older brothers and I went to the Bartlett school and most days we had to walk to school. Sometimes they would run ahead of me causing me to be late for school. My mother hated when the school called her. I wasn't the best dressed kid in school, teachers would give me bags of clothes to take home and it would be an insult to my mother. She would take the bags of clothes and throw them away as she yelled at me for, "looking so pitiful." Most of my haircuts were products of a plastic bowl being placed on my head and absence of baths meant I was one of the few kids pulled out of class and given a yellow envelope that stated, 'Your kid has lice.'

Things started to calm down, maybe because summer was over, school had started or because my mother had a new boyfriend and she was excited for us all to meet. We started doing a lot of things as a family; trips to the drive-in, beaches, Whalom amusement park and eating dinners every night. It wasn't long until I was asked to call him dad and when I didn't, my mother would remind me that I was a child of an asshole and how my real dad never loved me.

Soon my mother got a part time job working nights. Leaving my two brothers and myself to stay home with her new boyfriend who quickly moved in. He left for work in the morning, coming home in the afternoon to a cooked dinner so he could drive my mother to work and come back home to feed us supper. He was excited to put my brothers in anything they wanted, karate, boys club and he was more excited the first day he got to babysit me alone. He was only going to drop my brothers off at karate class and he would be right back. He told me not to get off the couch and I did what any five-year-old would do, I listened. I remained on the couch until he returned. He was so happy to babysit me, he talked about my dad and how sad he was that my dad had to die. He questioned me if I knew why my dad died and I shook my head letting him know my answer was no. He explained my dad died because he wasn't the right dad for me. He could tell he was confusing me, so he went to the kitchen to fetch me some dinner. Instead, he came back with an ice cream cone. Before handing me the ice cream cone, I had to promise not to tell anyone we had ice cream for dinner, so I promised. I was allowed to sit on the couch, watch television and eat ice cream for supper. Which is something my mother would never allow. While eating my ice cream he told me how he wanted to have a father/daughter relationship with me. He also told me about fathers keeping secrets with their daughters. "Like this ice cream," he said to me with a giggle. He was afraid God would take him like he took my real dad. He questioned me if I had secrets with my real dad and when I answered him, "No," he got all excited and yelled, "See that's why God took him." He told me to finish my ice cream and then we would clean up so we could share another secret.

He came back into the living room and sat next to me on the couch. He continued talking about wanting a father/daughter relationship with me and how we were starting one that very day when we shared the secret about having ice cream for supper. He insisted, "We do the father/daughter thing the right way so God won't take me like he took your real dad." He repeated himself numerous times as he grabbed my hand and placed it on his lap. He insisted, "This is what God wants." His grip got tighter as he explained God was watching us to see if we do the right secrets fathers do with their daughters. He unzipped his pants and forced my hand to touch his penis inside. I quickly screamed, "It's your pee," as I tried to get off the couch. He grabbed me so tight, shaking me as he yelled about God killing my mother and brothers if I didn't do his secret. He pulled my head towards him, squeezing so tight.

Next thing, my mother was pulling me from behind a chair in the living room where she found me crying hysterically. She was yelling at me for still being up and for giving her boyfriend a hard time while he watched me. I did wonder how my brothers were already home and in bed, why it was so late and what happened to me? My brother's bedroom was right next to the chair I was found crying behind. My mother carried me into bed asking why I was crying so hard. I told her I couldn't tell her because it was a secret and I didn't like the secret. She covered me with blankets, telling me to stop crying and get some sleep. Which is what I did.

A few days later on a school night and a day my mother had off of work, her boyfriend was already in bed sleeping while my brothers and I watched television in the living room with our mother. When it came time for our snack, she sent my brothers into the back hall where the snack cabinet was, telling them to be quiet and for me to get ready for bed first. When I was done changing into pajamas, I went back into the living room where my brothers were already eating their snack. I questioned my mother for my snack and she gave me the same instructions, telling me to be quiet. I walked silently through the kitchen and into the back hall. I quietly opened the snack cabinet door and was about to grab a box of scooter pies when my eyes opened wide as a hand reached from behind me and covered my mouth. A man's voice whispered in my ear, "Be quiet." As I was scooped into a dark place and something was shoved inside my mouth causing me to bite down. I heard the man yell as something whacked me upside my head causing me to fall to the floor. The moonlight shined into the room and as I turned my head, I noticed it was my mother's boyfriend, but I didn't understand what he was doing to me? He pulled my nightgown over my head, rubbing me with his hands and a heaviness I couldn't get off me. He was hurting me as he continued to touch my pee area causing me to squirm enough that something banged against the wall and made a loud bang. He jumped up, yanked me to my feet and ordered me to go straight to bed. I ran through the kitchen and straight into my bed where I cried myself to sleep. I wondered where my mother was, I had only left to get a snack. I didn't understand what her boyfriend did to me but I knew I didn't like it and I knew I was going to tell my mother.

The next morning my mother was in the kitchen, getting us our breakfast. I questioned her where her boyfriend was, she answered he was at work. I then asked her why she didn't look for me after I went for a snack. She answered she did but I was already in bed sleeping. I then told her, "I didn't get a snack because he grabbed me." She cut me off calling me a crybaby, how he already told her about it and how he was only trying to be funny. It was quickly forgotten as he continued to spoil us kids. Me with dolls and my brothers with racetracks and bikes. But he didn't forget when one Saturday morning my mother went out to run errands, leaving the three of us home with him.

I was in my brothers' room watching them play with their train and racetrack sets. Our mother's boyfriend came into the room asking if we all wanted ice cream. My brothers quickly said no because our mother didn't let us eat in our rooms. He insisted we could eat the ice cream in the bedroom while we played, so we all agreed we wanted ice cream. When he returned to the room, he only had two ice creams, one for each brother. He stated I was too young and had to eat my ice cream in the kitchen. I quickly changed my mind and didn't want one but he insisted I go in the kitchen because he already made the ice cream. I was a bit upset and thought it was unfair as I grabbed my doll and headed out of my brother's bedroom into the living room.

Once I was in the living room, he picked me up and swung me over one of his shoulders. He walked quickly through the living room, into the kitchen and a quick right turn into the bathroom. As he put me down, he put his finger to his mouth and said, "Shhhh." I was already feeling the fear, crying for my ice cream and wanting my mother by the time he shut the bathroom door. He handed me tissues telling me to stop crying. He was telling me he had a special ice cream for me and not enough to share with my brothers. I kept trying to get to the door but he would just hold me by my forehead, preventing me from going anywhere. He then grabbed me by both my arms, shaking me and asking me if I wanted my brothers to die? I answered him, "No." Then he told me I had to stop crying so he could go get my special ice cream. He was scaring me which made me cry more until he got angrier, asking me if I wanted him to walk out the door and kill my brothers so I would never see them again or did I want my ice cream? I wouldn't stop crying, so he started rushing me to answer, rushing me to stop crying or he was rushing out the door to kill my brothers. So, I stopped crying. I stopped crying long enough to see my doll laying on the bathroom floor and the moments it took him to return with a bottle and a belt in his hands. He placed the belt on top of the toilet, moved me away from the door and positioned me to stand in front of the toilet bowl. I tried moving away as he unzipped his pants exposing his penis causing me to cry louder and him angrily ordering me to be quiet. Forcing me to stand where he wanted me to be, he then poured chocolate syrup from the bottle onto his penis and yelled at me to lick it off. I kept crying and trying to get away, but he would just laugh and put me where he wanted me to stand.

He then grabbed the belt from the top of the toilet, licked chocolate syrup off his fingers as he looked at me. When suddenly one hand grabbed me by the back of my neck so hard, I squished down in pain. He flashed the belt into my face, his evil eyes, his face red in anger, his teeth clenched telling me if he ever felt my teeth again, he will whip me with the belt as he pulled my face into his syrup covered penis. I refused to open my mouth and his grip got tighter. He kept shoving and pushing my face into him as much as I cried and tried to squirm away. I was crying hysterically by the time he pulled his pants up quickly and wet a face cloth to wipe my

1975-1982 Lowell Massachusetts

face. Wetting it again before handing it to me, walking out the bathroom door and closing it behind him. I washed my face but was still crying and breathing heavy when the bathroom door opened and it was my mother. She questioned why I was crying but before I could answer her, she yelled at me to get out of the bathroom.

The kitchen floor was full of groceries as I walked across the kitchen to my bedroom. I heard my mother's boyfriend tell my mother that I had a fever and refused to take medicine as the reason why I was crying. I immediately yelled, "No it wasn't that," but I was cut off by my mother who yelled at me to get in my room.

Shortly afterwards, my mother came into my room and questioned why he made me cry so much. I told my mother, "He carried me in the bathroom." I told her he said he was going to kill my brothers. She questioned me, "Did he hurt you?" I nodded my head yes and that made my mother mad. She yelled at me that I was being a crybaby, I didn't appreciate a good father and I was a troublemaker. I tried to explain, but she said things that made it seem to be my fault. So many things went through my mind that day, I couldn't understand what I did wrong, I was barely six years old.

I continued being a kid, playing outside at the sand piles or running around the park. One day I heard a lady say my name, "Catherine." I knew immediately it was my grandmother and she was mad I was running around the park unsupervised. She had my brothers get my mother as we walked to her row of brick apartments. She always had snacks, drinks and a room full of stuffed animals. When my mother showed up, they yelled at each other. She was upset I had no supervision and my mother was mad because I was caught being outside alone. I returned home with my mother to a place where I was becoming afraid of the man who I would not call dad. As often as my mother would ask me to, I wouldn't call him dad.

My school started calling my mother at home about me always falling asleep in class. Teachers were asking me about the clothes they gave me and I would tell them I gave the bags to my mother. One teacher gave me brand new dresses with store tags still on them. I was so excited to wear them but my mother took them back to school and threw a fit over the teacher insulting her. Then one day my mother questioned me, "Why do you keep falling asleep in school?" I answered her because her boyfriend keeps coming into my room and waking me up. I told her he sits on my bed in his underwear and makes my hand touch his pee, but she cut me off, yelling how I make a mountain out of a molehill.

I would be on my way out the back door to play in the yard and he would come out of his bedroom, scoop me up and bring me into his bedroom he shared with my mother. He would throw me on his bed, hold my body down with his legs and both my hands with one of his hands. He would pull down my pants, lift my shirt up, rub himself against me, force me to touch him and force my face into his penis. He said it was me who was making him hurt me, because I kept fighting him and I wouldn't listen, causing him to squeeze me tighter and harder until I calmed down enough for him to finish. If my mother was or came home, then he'd whack me with the belt so I had a reason for my puffy crying face. Sometimes he would squeeze me so tight, I would awake already in my bed, those were the nights I did not get hit with the belt. I would tell my mother how he made me smell a cloth and then I'd awake in my bed. But she never cared to bother.

One time my mother couldn't find me in the yard and the cops were called. I awoke to a houseful of firefighters and police officers. My mother laughed about it, claiming I was in bed the whole time. When I tried to tell her, I wasn't in my bed and how it was her boyfriend who put me there. Her hand went over my mouth as she joked with the people in the home. The officers and firemen quickly left once I was found and my life continued. The fear of my mother's boyfriend was becoming constant. My mother would ask me to stop being mean to him and remind me of all the nice things he buys for us all. He would remind me this is what fathers and daughters do. From coming into my room, bringing me into the bathroom, pulling me into his and my mother's bedroom and telling me that I would get used to it.

It wasn't long until my mother was in the hospital having a baby. I remember looking out the window for the stork flying in with a pink or blue

1975-1982 Lowell Massachusetts

blanket. My brothers stayed elsewhere and I was left home to stay with my mother's boyfriend. The baby was already born when he took me to the hospital so I could see my mother and my new baby sister. When we got to the hospital, we were informed I was too young to be a visitor. I was upset and had to sit in a room until he was done visiting my mother. A nurse sat with me, giving me juice, jello and a freeze pop. She was nice as she questioned me about my mother and baby sister. That's when I got upset and cried out, "Is he going to make a secret with her too?" The nurse was stunned, stood up and walked out the door. She immediately returned with other adults. I didn't understand the trouble I had caused. There was a big commotion amongst adult's when my mother's boyfriend returned insisting, he would never hurt me. After being left in the room for a long while, they all came back into the room and explained to me that it was all a big misunderstanding. And just like that I was allowed to leave with him. He held my hand all through the hospital, the parking lot and into his truck where he angrily told me of the trouble, I was in for causing trouble with him.

He sent me straight to my room telling me to go to bed. Shortly afterwards he came into my room and reminded me of the trouble I caused. He ordered me out of my bed and told me to lean over. He continued to whack me with his belt onto my buttocks as he yelled, "This one's for not listening," "This one's for being a crybaby," "This one's for giving me a hard time," and he went on and on. Guess he whacked me one too many times. When my mother came home from the hospital, she noticed I wasn't sitting right and questioned what was wrong. I told her my bum hurt and she quickly pulled me towards her, pulled my pants down enough to expose my bruised and swelled buttocks. Suddenly there was a lot of yelling and fighting. My mother was fighting with her boyfriend because he was in trouble for hurting me. She came into my room shortly afterwards to tell me, "How sorry he was." Telling me it was my fault I made him so mad by not behaving or listening to him when she was in hospital having my baby sister. She then assured me she wasn't going back to work now that the baby was here and for me just to yell for her if he does hurt me again.

She had me sit on a tube seat until the bruises healed. I soon found my way back to my grandmother's and would walk there often. Each and every time she was upset, I was without an adult. Then calling for an older person to come get me.

My grandmother told me I was named after her and another grandmother on her side of the family. Anytime I knocked on her door or got called in when she saw me running by unsupervised, she was always full of hugs, drinks, snacks and a stuffed animal to take home. Sometimes she would tell me I just missed my siblings or my dad. I didn't know what a sibling was and I thought she meant my mother's boyfriend was my dad. I wanted to yell at her, "He's not my dad," but I liked being at my grandmother's and I didn't want to get her mad at me.

My brothers and I would walk all over the acre section of Lowell. Through alleyways and short cuts through yards to railroad tracks, city hall, George's pizza, a variety store or sneak me into the North Common swimming pool. With our mother being home full time, we would go for long walks throughout the city of Lowell with the baby in a stroller. I remember thinking I was so grown up when my mother let me push the stroller. I got to hold my baby sister a few times at home as long as I was sitting down. Soon we were back in school at the Bartlett and shortly afterwards my mother had my brothers and I signed up for religious education classes at St. Patrick's school on Adams Street. My mother's boyfriend tried hard to win back my trust. I wouldn't look at him, I ran by him anytime he walked into a room I was in. My mother would tell me he was sad because I kept avoiding him. One day after catholic Sunday school he came into my bedroom where I was doing my homework. I immediately started to yell, "Get out." But he insisted he just wanted to talk. He promised he wouldn't hurt me. He instantly started crying because I wasn't being the daughter God wanted me to be. He told me the next time I go to catholic Sunday school, "Ask your teacher if God sends secret messages," he insisted. He was sad as he explained to me that God was going to take him like God took my father. He explained that God appointed him to be my new dad and how I was being a bad daughter. He didn't hurt me that day, he just really messed with my six-year-old head. When I went to my next catholic Sunday school class, I raised my hand and questioned my teacher, "Does God send secret messages?" The teacher answered me, "Yes." My mother's boyfriend had to shake the teacher's answer out of me. It wasn't long until he was back to using his belt and his evilness on me. Showing me photos, he took of me naked with tape over my mouth, being put to sleep with a cloth over my mouth and filming me with double reel film. I screamed in horror while he laughed so loud.

My mother was becoming suspicious of rides he took me on as they were becoming more frequent, taking longer and I returning home crying every time which was causing arguments between my mother and him. Sometimes my mother showed concern, sometimes she got mad at me because they argued over me and sometimes, she would sit next to me to explain, "He mixed-up his adult playing with you," she told me one day. Telling me again to yell if he does something I don't like. I yelled anytime he tried to grab me and by the time my mother came into the room, it was passed off as a joke to them and I was teased for being more of a baby than my own baby sister was. Because I didn't know how to be quiet was his reason for using tape over my mouth, smacking my head and squeezing my face while yelling at me, "This is what God wants."

During the spring of 1977 the attacks were becoming eviler and more often than before. There were so many times he got so mad because he had to force me and he wanted me to just do what he wanted me to do. He would get angrier the more I gave him a hard time. He would sit on top of me, squeezing my arms with his legs, ordering me to lick his penis and smacking it across my face. I would squirm and move enough to slide through his legs but he would just grab me, flip me back onto the bed and force me to watch him or help him masturbate. One day he took the tape off my mouth and told me to scream for help. So, I screamed as loud as I could. He then screamed with me as he laughed and slowly walked over to the wall, he had me cornered in. He placed the tape back over my mouth as he laughed into my face, "No one's home." No one was home, my mother left me home with him. He would tell me, "Can't use the cloth all the time."

As he informed me, "How will you learn if you sleep through it all?" He would remind me, "This is what God wants." He would threaten me about telling his secret that he called, "Our secret." That day when my mother got home, I asked her why she left me home with him. She answered she left me home because I was sick. When I tried to tell her about what her boyfriend did to me, she was too busy and shunned me away. I was always hurting, whether it was my hands and wrists from being held too tight, my head from being squeezed or my body from sliding through his grip and the fear I had towards the man who lived with us. It was all an excuse my mother used saying, "I was just a kid who got hurt a lot."

It wasn't long until a teacher at school pulled me from my chair and away from the other kids in the classroom. She lifted my shirt up to expose my back area, then walked me to the principal's office where she did the same and lifted my shirt. I was told to sit in a room while they called my mother and soon, she was at the school. There was always a lot of screaming when it came to my mother and that day was no exception. Soon social workers were visiting our home and with each visit the person always wanted to talk to me. They would ask questions about my brothers, baby sister, my school or my dolls. After talking with me, the social worker would write something down in a booklet and then leave until the next visit. Sometimes it was the same social worker and sometimes it wasn't, but every time, I got a lecture from my mother about what to say and what not to say.

My mother had a car now and we would go visit her sister Claudette. We would do Easter egg hunts at her house on Easter Sunday. We also visited two of her friends, Theresa who had kids our age and Pauline who was a hairdresser with a son younger than us. One day I questioned my mother why she gave Pauline a kiss on the cheek every time we left her house and my mother answered that she was a longtime friend of hers. Her friend Theresa who we always visited had a set of twins our age, one boy and one girl. Theresa was a super nice lady who was always smiling, laughing and pinching our butts whenever she gave us a hug. She always had prizes for us and always fed us when we were there. One day while playing at Theresa's, I overheard my mother tell Theresa, "I think he is having fun with her."

I immediately got up from where I was playing and stood right at the table they were sitting at, waiting for more to be said. But my mother snapped at me, "Stop being nosey and go play."

Before we left to go home, Theresa gave me a hug, pulled me to the side and said, "I don't know what's going on with you but if someone hurts you, punch them back, ok?" Then she gave me another hug. Soon it was my first communion day. The morning started when my mother's boyfriend came into my room all excited about my big day and what it meant for him and I. He was having trouble getting inside of me and gave me a brown plastic cigar cover that he gave away after my baby sister was born. I wouldn't take it from his hands so he placed it on my bed. He was telling me he was helping me become a woman, how I was an older sister now and I got a pretty dress to wear. He kept telling me to practice putting the cigar tube where I pee and push it inside. Telling me to keep it under my pillow before he left my room as if he was the loving step father of the year. I got up, walked out of my room, straight to my mother and I handed her the cigar tube. "Where did you get that?" she questioned me. I told her from her boyfriend, she gave a look of disgust and walked into her bedroom where her boyfriend was.

I knew I was in a lot of trouble by the dirty looks I got as I waited in line outside of St Patrick's Church. Though my name is spelled Kathy Melon on my certificate, on that day in May 1977, I made my first communion and a party followed. There were a lot of people at the house, a lot of kids lived in the building and there was a first communion cake for me. There were gifts, cards with money inside and a loud commotion going on outside. I was still in my communion dress when I looked out the window and saw my uncle. I immediately booked it to the front door so I could see him but I was quickly stopped by my mother who was coming in from outside. "Is my uncle coming in?" I questioned my mother but she snapped at me, "No." Then she handed me another card with money in it.

A few days later I was getting ready to go shopping with the money given to me for making my first communion. I waited patiently in the kitchen for my mother but instead she told me, "He's taking you." I threw a fit, I didn't want to go, but she got so mad and ordered me to go shopping with her boyfriend. On our way to the store, he told me if I was a good girl then he wouldn't make me do what we usually did when we went for rides, which was forcing me to masturbate him or force my face into his penis. So, a good girl I was. Once we were at the store, he kept picking out toys for me to decide what I was buying. But I had no interest in picking a toy out with him next to me. He was becoming frustrated until I finally picked out a doll as I could tell he was becoming angry with me. When we were at the register, the cashier made a comment about my dad buying me a doll and I blurted out, "He's not my dad." Embarrassing him in the process.

On our way back home, it was a quiet ride. I wasn't even excited over the doll I just got myself. I just wanted to get home. He stopped the truck on a deserted road, turned the key of the truck off and proceeded to tell me that I had to be punished. "Do you know why you have to be punished?" he questioned me. I was already crying when I answered him, "No." He responded, "Because you weren't a happy fucking kid in the store." As he pulled me closer to him, grabbing my mouth with his hands and forcing it to stay open as he turned me trying to get his penis in my mouth.

I could feel the tears run down my face, the spit down my chin as I gagged and tried to move. His grip was too strong as he kept his hands prying my mouth open and putting his penis inside. Holding me by my neck after he released my mouth so I could watch him finish as he masturbated. He kept a roll of paper towels in his glove compartment that he used to clean me up with. When we got home that day, I whipped my new doll at my mother and yelled at her, "I hate you." Before running into my room where I cried. For the first time I blamed my mother for allowing her boyfriend to hurt me like he was. My mother came into my room a little while after I threw my new doll at her. She had the doll in her hand and out of the box as she came in waving the doll at me claiming how pretty she was. I didn't want it, so she then sat down on my bed where I was still crying. She again explained to me how sorry her boyfriend was for hurting me. I questioned her, "He told you?" She answered me, he did tell her everything. I questioned, "He told you what he makes me do?" She said, "Yes," as she explained, "He has a sickness and it was out of his control," she said. She also explained he was going to control it so he doesn't hurt me anymore.

It wasn't long before I was reminded how much trouble I was in for causing my mother to question him about what happened on that ride we took to spend my communion money. He would poke my head, bend my hand backwards, squeeze my head as he dangled me above the floor. All in an attempt to make me promise that I would not tell my mother on him again. Every time, whether he succeeded in the attack or not, if my mother was in the other room, he would open the bedroom door, throw me over his knee and whack me with his white leather belt. So my mother knew there was a reason why I was crying. Sometimes I ran out of the bathroom or bedroom crying hysterically and my mother was home. I do believe my older brothers were too young to understand what was happening to me, but my mother always knew.

I was instilled with fear, terror and the fact it kept happening. I was filmed with a double reel film; I was posed in photos as he joked about buying a new camera so he didn't get caught when he developed the film. I was threatened about being killed, about my brothers and mother being killed and about the ones he killed before me. He told me about a little girl right before me who wouldn't shut up so he stuffed her in a trash bag and, "Tossed her on the side of the road." he said so proudly. He warned me about kids in the service and how, "Everyone let's a kid go with a soldier." He was evil and used his strength against me. He would block me from running away from him. He would toss me like I was a rag doll. I would awake on my mother's bed with no clothes on, zip ties on my wrist and tape over my mouth. I would get smacked upside my head while he was sexually assaulting me. He would rub his sperm all over my body, telling me it was lotion. He would viciously and violently force his penis in my mouth, force my hands around his penis or force me to watch him as he masturbated.

As summer went by, I was still getting in trouble from my grandmother for roaming the North Common Park by myself. She would see me and I'd hear, "Catherine," and a bunch of mumbles under her breath. I'm sure it was about being without an adult. There was an arts and craft program at the park during the summer and my mother got in trouble as I was always showing up without an adult.

One day, I stepped on a piece of broken glass. It went through my flip flop and into my foot. One of the workers from the program had to carry me from the park to my home where my mother threw me in her car and drove me to the hospital. There was a lot of blood and I got a few stitches. I then spent the rest of the summer, healing from my stitches and being more available to my mother's boyfriend. No matter how many times my mother questioned me to call him dad, I would only call him by the name, "Him." He would bring me down into the cellar and violently attack me as I huddled down to the floor, one time a man yelled something and I ran as I limped, getting lost in the dark scary cellar. Another time I awoke on a stretcher as I was wheeled into a hospital corridor. Soon a nurse was telling me, "It was ok to say they hurt you." But just as quickly my mother came into the room yelling at the nurse to get away from me.

Soon there were boxes throughout the apartment as we were getting ready to move to a nicer and bigger home. There was a truck outside where my brothers and my mother's boyfriend were carrying boxes out to. Everyone was busy when my mother pulled me to the side because she wanted to talk with me. She questioned me again to call her boyfriend dad. Telling me he was really trying hard to be good to me and how he loves me. I was stubborn and refused to call him dad, I kept shaking my head no as my mother kept asking until I finally yelled, "He's not my dad, he's Dave." Just as he walked back into the house and gave me a dirty look when he heard me answer my mother. Dave and my brothers continued carrying boxes from the apartment to the truck.

That day was the first time I called my abuser by his name and the last time I called Fletcher Street my home as we packed up and moved across the city.

On the ride to our new home, I envisioned what it would look like. I imagined a huge house with a huge hallway and stairs that spiraled as it went up. I envisioned I had a pink bedroom with a white bed and bureau.

I envisioned a fairytale home with a huge yard and maybe some horses. But as we pulled onto our new street, I learned it was nothing like I had envisioned.

I could never imagine the house of horror that home would end up being to me.

Two
A House of Horrors

WE MOVED TO PLEASANT STREET, a street with many one- and two-family homes. Our new home was one that happened to house four apartments side by side to each other. Inside on the first floor as you walked into the hallway, it led you to the kitchen which led to a dining room, on through the living room and back into the hallway. It was a big circle of rooms. Along the wall on the left side of the hallway was a set of stairs leading up to three bedrooms and the bathroom. There was another set of stairs which led up to the attic and two more bedrooms with a small hallway in between them. My sister and I were put in the bedroom by the bathroom while my brothers were put in the bedroom by the stairs. My mother and Dave got the master bedroom and one room in the attic would be used as our playroom. My sister's first birthday was held later in the month of August, weeks after her birthday of August 9th due to the move. School started really quickly and instead of going to the Bartlett, we were now going to the Rogers school. Because we lived too far, my mother had to drive us to and from school every day. I was an extremely quiet kid in school and always the youngest in my class due to my birthday being in December.

Back at home, the only bathroom in the home was upstairs and it had two windows in it. One you could look into my mother's room and the other you could look into my bedroom by standing on the tub. Dave would step on the tub and watch me through the window. Whether he was taunting me with knocks on the window, doing sexual gestures with his mouth or letting me know he was watching me. I would scream and yell for my mother who would yell at me for yelling. She would insist he was sleeping in bed and couldn't have been in the bathroom, I was making it up or yell at me for waking up my baby sister. Dave would come into my room telling me he had a duty to make me a woman, that it was his job to make me into a woman and he was only doing what he was supposed to be doing.

It was easy to get rid of him when he came into my room because I'd just scream and my mother would come upstairs yelling at me for screaming. I would awake to him whispering in my ear, "Ohhhh Cathy." I would scream, I always screamed as I did when I found him hiding in my closet after I took a tub. My mother was so mad at me. She moved my baby sister into her bedroom, my oldest brother to the bedroom in the attic, my other older brother got my bedroom and I was moved to the bedroom by the stairs. She didn't move the bedrooms because Dave kept coming in my room or watching me through the window. She moved them because I kept waking up my baby sister and so I couldn't accuse Dave of looking through the bathroom window anymore. Her words to me were, "See, solved that didn't I?" I looked at her strangely and confused as I decorated my new bedroom.

Not long afterwards, Dave called my name as I was going down the stairs from my bedroom. He found something of mine in one of the boxes he unpacked. I quickly went over to his bedroom doorway to see what it was. He handed me that brown plastic cigar tube he gave me on Fletcher Street, asking me if I remembered what he told me to do with it. I answered him that I did remember and he then told me to put it in a secret place, telling me we would talk more about it later. I went downstairs to where my mother was and I handed her the plastic cigar tube, asking her to tell her boyfriend to stop giving it to me and that I didn't want it. She took it from my hands, said, "Oh boy," and that was the end of that. For now, anyways.

We would take visits to Dave's sister's house, sometimes staying late which caused my mother to be mad at Dave for driving drunk with us all in the car. He never did come for the visits we took to my aunt's or my mother's friend's house. We started to visit another one of my mother's sister's, our Aunt Jackie and Uncle Bob. It caused me to question about my uncle but my mother would just shoot me away, often complaining about my grandmother and telling me, "She is being a nag about seeing you." We visited my mother's hairdresser friend again because I needed a haircut. Pauline was told to give me a shaved pixie style haircut and she got upset it would make me look like a boy, but my mother didn't want to hear it. Pauline took me to the back of the hair salon and showed me pictures from a magazine of different hair styles and asked if I liked the feathered style cut, which I did. So that was the haircut I got and I loved it until we walked to the front of the hair salon. My mother was waiting and she yelled at Pauline for disobeying her wishes. My mother then yelled at me the whole way home, telling me how ugly my new haircut was.

AT home, just going to the bathroom gave Dave a chance to catch me alone. He came in one day as I was sitting on the toilet. He shut the door behind him and forced my face into his unzipped pants, causing me to fall off the toilet and pee on the floor. My screams caused my mother to come upstairs and she yelled at me about the mess. She returned with paper towels and threw them at me telling me to clean up the floor. As I told her what Dave had done, she slapped me across the face and told me to stop with my ridiculous stories. Days later I was in my bedroom when Dave came to the doorway, "Let's go," he said to me when I looked up at him. I guess I assumed my mother was home because I got right up, not thinking of the horror he puts me through. I went out of my bedroom, walking past him as he walked behind me and I headed for the stairs thinking that's where he wanted me to go. He grabbed me by my shoulders before I was able to make a step onto the stairs, he turned me towards the direction of his bedroom and escorted me inside as he shut the door. I walked in and saw a bottle of chocolate syrup on my mother's bureau resting next to a stack of napkins and a wet face cloth. The same stuff he had on Fletcher Street.

I immediately turned around and tried to run out the room, but the door was closed and he wouldn't allow it. I started to cry, begging him, "Please no." He grabbed me by the front of my throat, squeezing as I grabbed onto his hands in an attempt to make him stop. He would not stop until I shook my head yes as he continued to ask in an evil angered face, "You going to keep our secret?" When he let loose of my neck, he gave me tissues to wipe my tears. I wouldn't stop crying so he smacked me upside my head, causing me to fall onto the floor. He then picked me up and forced his chocolate syrup covered penis in my mouth. I gagged and tried to get away. He felt my teeth causing him to smack me again. When he was finished, he cleaned himself up, wiped my face with the wet face cloth and joked about how he would have to find a way not to make a mess when using the chocolate syrup. I was still crying as he looked at me laughing hysterically about the mess he made. Then he grabbed me tightly by my jaw and told me God would make him kill my brothers, baby sister and mother if I didn't learn to, "Shut the fuck up," he angrily said.

My brothers and I were adjusting to our new home, new school, making new friends and being kids. Soon it was the blizzard of 1978, schools were canceled and I walked around the neighborhood with my brothers seeing who needed help with shoveling. Day after day of shoveling. Many times, I walked with my brothers to go sledding at Fort Hill and Shedd Park. My brothers would hop cars by grabbing a car bumper as the car drove by and sledding with their feet as they hung on. Sometimes they got upset they had to take me along but most of the time they were pretty cool about me going, waiting for me as I fell behind walking. One day during winter vacation I went downstairs and headed towards the kitchen when everything went dark. I was grabbed from behind; my mouth was being covered by what would be Dave's arm as he held me in front of him and carried me down into the cellar. Once in the cellar, he tossed me onto the floor. I saw the bottle of chocolate syrup as he grabbed it, along with a cloth while I tried to get up and run. But he placed his foot onto my hand, pressing down hard to prevent me from moving as I screamed in pain. He then quickly grabbed me by my neck and ordered me in his angered evil face to, "Shut the fuck up." He pried my mouth open with his hands as my body twisted, I gagged and cried but his strength was too strong for me. He blamed me for getting hurt, saying over and over again that it was me who caused so much trouble in the home. When he was finished with me, he kicked me as I cried on the cellar floor before dragging me over to a pole where he tied a chain around me and made me sit there and think about the trouble, I cause him. He put a piece of tape over my mouth before he headed upstairs. I spent the next hour or so, crying as I sat chained to the pole.

When he came back down the cellar stairs, he unhooked the chain he wrapped around me, then said, "Go," as he motioned me to head upstairs. I ran but he stopped me before I got to the stairs, grabbing my throat and threatening me to keep my mouth shut. Once I saw my mother, I approached her and told her, "Mom, he dragged me down the cellar." But like many times before, she walked away.

With snow piles still higher than most houses, my mother took me for a ride one day and pulled up to some brick apartments off of Salem Street. She handed me some papers with a pen and said as she pointed her finger, "Knock on that door right there and tell your stupid father to sign this." I looked at her confused, "My dad?" I questioned her. "Yes," she answered as she rushed me out of the car. "But you said he was dead," I said to my mother as she yelled at me to hurry up because we had to get home to my baby sister. I got out of the car and walked to the door she pointed at. I was so mad and so confused. I knocked and a woman opened the door so excited to see me. I walked inside and saw my dad laying on a couch. Before he could say anything, I said, "My mother wants you to sign this," as

I showed him the stack of papers in my hands. He had trouble getting up off the couch. He grabbed a cane, walked by me and out the door to where my mother was in her car. There was a lot of yelling outside, while inside the woman introduced herself as my stepmother and told me my dad has been looking for me and she was so happy I was there. My dad came back inside, picked me up and hugged me while asking if I wanted to sleep over that weekend and I said yes. On the way home I told my mother I was sleeping over and gave her the phone number he wrote down to give her. I also questioned her why she said he was dead, but she just went on about how he was no better than the father I had at home.

    I was slowly becoming a stranger in my own home. I was only eight years old and I was petrified of my mother's boyfriend, the man I now called Dave. I was in my bedroom one day reading a book I got from the RIF bus (Reading is Fundamental) at my school. It was a Judy Blume book I was reading when Dave walked into my room as I quickly screamed for him to get out. He stormed at me and I awoke laying on the foot of my mother's bed. I quickly sat up and just as quickly Dave grabbed me by my head, picking me up off the bed and warning me about telling my dad about him, "Your dad and I are friends, did you know that?" he questioned me as he dropped me back onto the bed, laughing about the phone call he just had with my dad. "You tell him about our secret, he calls me, you come home, your family will be dead and it will be all your fault," he continued to threaten me as he paced back and forth at the foot of the bed. We heard the downstairs front door shut and he quickly wiped his hand across my face in an attempt to clear the tears I was crying. He then opened his bedroom door to see my mother coming up the stairs. As he rushed me out the door, my mother was walking toward her bedroom and I heard her say, "What's her problem now?" I almost walked into her as I headed back to my bedroom where I saw the book I was reading still on my bed with a white cloth, stained with a blue spot laying right next to it.

    I grabbed the cloth and stood at my doorway waiting for my mother to come out of her bedroom. When she finally did, I called her to my room and told her, "Mom I was reading a book and he used this cloth again to put me to sleep." But she immediately headed back out of my bedroom and towards the stairs. I chased her out of my room and yelled as she started down the stairs, "Mom, he put me on your bed." Dave then came out of his bedroom, hearing what I hollered to my mother. He cornered me against the wall and threatened me about not going to my dad's the coming weekend.

The weekend was finally here and I was super excited. I remember feeling like I was wanted, like someone actually cared for me. I had my bag packed waiting patiently for my mother to drive me to my dad's house. I was ready to go before Dave got out of work, but my mother wasn't ready to drive me. She wanted to wait until Dave got home, then we had to wait until she cooked supper and then I had to go make sure my room was cleaned. I headed upstairs to recheck and make sure my room was clean, and it was. As I headed back out of my bedroom, I was stopped when an arm pulled me against the wall, it was Dave. "Remember our secret," he threatened me as I yelled, "Leave me alone." I then ran down the stairs as fast as I could. I was really excited to go to my dad's, I was going to tell him about Dave, about my mom telling me he was dead and I was going to tell him everything. That is until my mother said to me on the ride over, "Don't forget what Dave said to you." My eight-year-old brain filled with so many questions and one that stuck with me the whole weekend at my dad's, 'Was my dad and Dave friends?' I knew then, I would not be telling my dad about Dave or about anything that my mother said or did.

My dad took me over to my godfather's house and to the Sac Club where he knew a lot of people and I had my first orange ice cream soda. Then we went back to my dad's where me and other kids from the neighborhood formed a line inside my dad's house. Starting at the front door, up the stairs and through the bedroom window where we slid outside into the huge blizzard of 1978 snow pile that was right below. It was a lot of fun jumping into the snow pile until I fell right through to the bottom and my dad had to call the fire department to come help get me out. Everyone was laughing and I thought I was in trouble but my only punishment was a hot cup of cocoa and my dad who couldn't stop laughing about how he could see and hear me but the snow just sucked me in. At bedtime my dad wanted to bring me up to bed but when I got nervous, I asked if my stepmother could bring me instead. She did, she tucked me in and left a night light on for me. The next morning, I headed down the stairs when I overheard my dad telling my stepmother that something wasn't right with me. I say sorry too much, I was too jumpy and he was mad that he had to win my trust back. They knew I heard them when they saw me standing at the bottom of the stairs looking at them. My stepmother made me breakfast and we spent the day playing board games, card games, watching television and hanging in the bedroom that was mine for the weekend. I was scared my dad was going to attack me once I trusted him again.

On Sunday morning as we waited for my mother to pick me up, my dad was sitting in his chair when he grabbed me from behind and pulled me down to sit on his lap. He wrapped his arms around me causing me to scream. I jumped off of his lap and ran to the door. My stepmother stopped me and hugged me as she assured me my dad didn't mean to scare me. They wanted to talk to my mother when she arrived but she quickly drove away when I got in the car. On the ride home my mother questioned me about my weekend and I told her about the snow pile, my godfather and I questioned her if my dad came back to life to be a father like Dave was, if my dad wanted a father/daughter relationship with me? She answered that all fathers were the same and laughed at me for thinking my dad was some kind of a special dad that made him different from other dad's. Thinking my dad was going to do to me what Dave does, I told my mother I didn't want to go back there again. Back at home, Dave was getting us involved with talking on his citizens band radio and taking us on rides to New Hampshire so he could look for a camper to buy. My mother got a job at Capitol Warehouse working nights and weekends. My brothers were allowed to stay out later but I had to come in earlier because I was younger and had to help Dave with my baby sister whose crib was in his and my mother's bedroom. He would get me to play with my sister then he would close his door, approach me from behind and taunt me to get away as he blocked me from doing so. All while laughing as he unzipped his pants and exposed himself. He grabbed me by my neck, told me to stop crying and to be quiet. Insisting this was what God wanted and getting angrier the more I cried. Holding me down with his legs or by sitting on me as he would pour chocolate syrup over his penis demanding I keep my mouth open as he continued to push my face into him. He claimed he was being nice when he only wanted me to use my hands as he would pry my hands to stay open and force me to masturbate him. He got angrier with every hard time I gave him by forcing my mouth to stay shut, keeping my hand closed, hitting, kicking and always trying to get away from him.

Soon it was trips to Salisbury beach, Bensons Animal Farm and the drive-ins again. The only one's obvious to my fear of Dave was my mother and he, himself. My mother made repeated comments that I should go hold his hand or give him a hug and then she would get mad when I didn't, calling me a spoiled brat. I went to summer camp twice in the summer of 1978 and like the trip to my weekend sleepover at my dad's, Dave warned, threatened and reminded me of the consequences should I tell anyone about the secret he kept with me.

The first trip to summer camp, my mother and Dave drove me to Zayres department store parking lot where big yellow school buses were picking up kids by our age group and driving us off to our destination called summer camp. There were a lot of kids at camp, we all slept in a wide-open room lined with bunk beds. I learned how to make sailboats out of paper, I learned camping songs and I learned how to roast marshmallows on a twig from a tree. We went swimming, hiking, had a scavenger hunt and watched movies on a big white screen that was set up inside the rec hall.

My mother was called and talked about the screams I did while sleeping, but it was summed up to me just being a kid away from home for the first time. Once the trip at camp was over, we all piled into those big yellow school buses and headed back to Zayres parking lot where parents were waiting on their kids as my mother was waiting on me by her car. I saw kid's running to their parent's and so I did the same. I ran to where my mother was standing, I was all excited to tell her about my summer camp but as soon as I ran to her she grabbed my bag and rushed me into the car.

After driving away, I was about to tell her all the fun I had but she snapped at me, "They called telling me all about the crybaby you were." With no reply to my mother's comment the ride home remained a quiet one. Back at home during summertime 1978 there were a lot of kid's playing on Pleasant Street as I was gradually meeting them all.

Dave wanted to talk to me one day as he escorted me into his and my mother's bedroom. I started to cry as he assured me, "I'm not going to hurt you, I just want to talk." He would only talk if I stopped crying. So, with a pout on my face, I stopped crying and waited for what he wanted to say. I waited as he paced back and forth in his bedroom. I waited, he paced, I waited and waited as he paced and paced. Until he turned his back to me and just as quickly turned around as he questioned, "You know what?" He grabbed me by the bottom of my jaw, pulling me off the bed and slamming me onto the floor. Like a ball that didn't bounce, my body slammed onto the floor. My head hurt in pain as he kneeled over me, squeezing my jaw while questioning, "Did you tell anyone at camp, did you open your big fucking mouth?" he angrily questioned me as he squeezed my jaw so hard all I could do was shake my head no, but he wanted me to say it. He loosened the grip he had on my jaw so I was able to speak, "No, no one," I answered. He then stood up and grabbed my hand to help me stand up. He looked at me, put his hand on my head and said, "See that's how to be a good girl." He then told me to go play as he opened the bedroom door to let me out.

It was now time to go on my second round of summer camp, this time it was only my mother who drove me to Zayres parking lot to meet the yellow buses that would transport us kid's back to the same camp I went to just a few weeks earlier. I knew my mother would get mad at me, frustrated with me, disgusted in me and was already tired of me telling her what Dave did and was doing to me. So, on the ride to Zayres parking lot I decided to make a different approach to my mother. Sitting in the passenger seat as we drove through downtown, I wanted to tell her again about being attacked by Dave and so I said, "Mom he's still doing that stuff to me." By the time the last word came out of my mouth, my mother was already yelling at me, "How ridiculous you sound," "What would he want with a kid?" "Jesus Christ Cathy," "Come on huh," my mother continued being disgusted with me. When we got to Zayres parking lot my mother told me to, "Keep your mouth shut about your stupid stories," "No one needs to hear it," she continued. Also telling me to have fun and reminding me, "At least you don't have to worry about him," she said in a motherly way. I got in the bus where I headed for my second trip to summer camp.

My second trip to camp was not as much fun as the first time. Not because I was home sick, not because it wasn't fun to be there, not because kid's or the staff were mean to me. It was because my mother was called in for a meeting just two days after I arrived. I was outside playing with the other kid's when I saw my mother pull up in the office parking lot. I ran over to the fence that separated us kids from the parking lot, "What are you doing here?" I questioned my mother after she got out of her car and saw me standing at the fence. "Because you're a crybaby," she responded with a look of disappointment in me. I just looked away and ran off to go play with the other kids. My name was quickly called as I was motioned by camp staff to follow them. I was taken to the main office and taken into a room where my mother and camp staff were sitting. My mother was called due to my screaming and bad dreams that were disrupting the other kids in the sleeping quarters. My mother succeeded in convincing the staff that my bad dreams were from watching scary movies on television that I wasn't supposed to watch or from playing hide and seek at home with my brothers and how they often jumped out from hiding to scare me. I was given another chance to stay at camp and before my mother left, I was already outside playing with the other kids. It wasn't until bedtime when a girl who slept in the bunk bed next to me told me about waking her up the night before. "Are you homesick?" she questioned me. I answered her, "No." She told me about my screaming but I didn't believe her because I assumed the screams would wake me up also. Then we did what eight-year-olds are told to do at bedtime, we went to sleep.

I was still screaming in my sleep and one night I awoke to two staff members running to me as I sat up in bed. They took me over to their sleeping quarters and set me up a bed to lay down on. "That's not normal," I heard the staff member's talking to each other. They saw I was hearing everything they were saying so they sat down with me to explain how I was having some really bad nightmares. They covered me up with a blanket and had me fall asleep in the area the camp counselors and staff slept. Once we woke for breakfast, I was taken to the eating area of the camp where I ate breakfast with the other kids. When breakfast was over the other kid's got to go off to do camp stuff while I was escorted to the main office once again. I was taken into the same room I was in when my mother was called in days earlier, but my mother wasn't in the room. It was an older woman and she was dressed like a nun. She wanted to talk to me about the nightmares I was having as I was still disrupting the other kids while they slept. She questioned me a lot about my life, "Do you like school? Do you have pets at home? What's your favorite outside game? Is there anything you want to tell me that may cause you to have these nightmares?" As the older woman continued to question me, I continued to answer her, "Yes I like school, yes I have a cat, kickball was my favorite outside game and my mother's boyfriend makes me keep secrets." The woman left the room for a bit as I sat in the chair I was told to sit in when I first walked into the room. I was watching my feet dangle above the floor when in came the woman, my mother and Dave. They had called my mother to have another meeting and this time she showed up with Dave.

I listened to my mother as she explained to the lady and other staff members how the secret's I was referring to was about all the times Dave let me have ice cream without telling my brothers or staying up later at night after my brothers were sent to bed or all the snacks and special toys I would receive and not my brothers. "Isn't that right Cathy?" Dave questioned me as all eyes went on me and all I could do was just shake my head yes. I was sent home that day with my mother and Dave after being told I was, "Too young to be away from home." During the car ride home, my mother continued to call me a brat, a troublemaker, a liar and telling me I was grounded as soon as we got home. All while trying to smack me with her hand from the front passenger seat she was sitting in as she kept throwing her arm to the backseat attempting to smack me. Because seatbelts were not a law in 1978 it was a lot easier for me to dodge my mother's whacks as I was able to maneuver myself from being in her arm's length. It was a long ride from the summer camp place but I knew by Dave's quietness, I was also in a lot of trouble with him. After being home from summer camp for a few days I found out just how upset Dave was about my second trip at camp. I experienced a torture and fear no animal, never mind a human or child should ever have to go through. With no cloth putting me to sleep, Dave violently stripped my clothes off and stretched my legs apart, no matter how much it hurt. He squeezed my head with one hand as he rubbed his other hand and face all over my private parts. He forced my mouth open by pulling at my jaw and forcing his penis inside my mouth. All while I gagged, cried and tried to get away. He insisted it was all my fault because he had to hurt me.

    I soon became friends with the girl next door whose name was Sue. We played outside in front of the house, in her house, in her backyard and I would even sleep over her house. She never played in my house nor did she ever sleep over. Dave would act normal around other people; he would refer to me as his daughter out in public and I knew the consequences of correcting him that I was not his daughter. So, I wouldn't say a thing when I heard him call me his daughter out in public places like Whalom Park where he took us every summer for work outings the company Shaw Print, he worked for, held every year. But behind closed doors or in his truck, Dave was not a nice man. He would take me and my baby sister out for rides to a road lined with trees or to the top of Fort Hill Park. He would turn my sister's old fashioned car seat and give her toys to play with. Then he would make me masturbate him as he flicked my head with his fingers, letting me know how worthless to my family I was because I was always crying and giving him a hard time. My mother made me go for a ride with Dave one day because he was buying me new shoes for school. It wasn't the same employee but it was the same shoe store he took me to before, Anderson Little on Plain Street. I drew attention to the workers there due to my reaction being there with Dave. I didn't say anything, I didn't do anything but they questioned Dave numerous times asking if I was ok. Soon it was the first day of school at the Edith Rogers school. Each grade had a line, each line had a teacher with a list of names, but no teacher had my name. So, they put me in a class as the principal went to figure out where I belonged. That took over a month.

One day, I was called out of class and sent to the principal's office where I sat in a chair outside her office door. For a kid a few minutes is like forever. Many teachers went in and out of the principal's door all saying hello to me. But then I heard it, a slamming of a door out in the hallway and a loud voice came storming into the area I was sitting in, it was my mother. She went into the principal's office where I heard my mother bitching and complaining to them. Then she stormed out of the office, the area I was sitting in and the school. A while later the principal came out of her office. "What are you still doing here?" she questioned me. She then called my mother to come back to the school and get me. My mother had my age a year older at the school making me be in a grade higher than I was supposed to be in. My mother played that card well throughout my whole childhood.

I stayed home from school with my mother and baby sister for almost two weeks while my mother worked on getting me to another school. It wasn't long until I started at the Oakland elementary school on Sycamore Street where I took a bus to and from school at the corner of Sherman and High Street. My mother was still working, my brothers still got to stay out later than me and I was still being called in early. Dave acted nice to me in front of others as he continued his ways with me. Whether I was going to the bathroom, brushing my teeth or put in the bathroom by Dave, he would force me to touch his penis, force me to open my mouth or force me to take a bath and pose in different positions. Each time running back to his bedroom so he could see how I looked through the window and if I moved, cried or tried to get out, he would come in and put me back into the tub, hurting me as he squeezed my neck so hard threatening to snap it. He squeezed my neck so hard one time because I wasn't listening and he was tired of telling me over and over again to stop crying. He squeezed so tight that he didn't have to squeeze my neck in the tub again because I was now listening. I would have to pose for him so he could take pictures until the bubbles in the tub disappeared, fanning the pictures in the bathroom and showing them to me when it developed minutes later. He would continue to threaten me of coming home from school and finding my brothers, sister and mother dead in order to stop me from telling anyone at school.

Every time Dave let me out of their bedroom after he attacked and terrorized me, I always walked out with puffy eyes from crying and heavy breathing from the gasp of breath I was trying to make through the pain and shame I was walking in. He would threaten me from going into the bathroom to wash him off of me as he called his sperm, he rubbed all over me, "Lotion." "Got to save money on paper towels," he would say smiling as if he is that stepfather of the year again. I would cry myself to sleep, begging God to come get me but life kept going. I'd wake up, catch the bus to school and try to be outside or over a friend's house if my mother was at work.

The only thing that sucked was, I was only eight years old. When your told to, "Come in now," when you're playing outside or, "Let's go," when you're playing in the playroom or, "Time for bed." There is no choice for an eight-year-old to make but to listen to what you're told. We were already living on Pleasant Street a little over a year and Dave had attacked me in the cellar, bathroom, the tub, my bedroom and the bedroom he shared with my mother enough times to make me, an eight-year-old girl so extremely petrified of him.

On a night my mother was working at Capitol Warehouse, Dave didn't bother me as I played. Even when he came downstairs to tell me it was almost my bedtime, get pjs on and to brush my teeth, he was being nice about it. As I headed back down the stairs from getting ready for bed, Dave called my name in a loud whisper sound, "Pssst Cathy," he said. I pretended not to hear him and continued down the stairs. I wasn't even at the bottom steps when I heard him call my name in a loud manner, "Cathy." I looked up to see him motioning me upstairs as he stood over the railing in the upstairs hallway. I froze still as I looked upward towards him. Giving me the evil eye and warning me to get up the stairs and in his room before I caused him to wake up my baby sister. By the time I got to the doorway of his and my mother's bedroom, he was already laying on his side of the bed in only his underwear. My baby sister was sleeping in her playpen, the shades to the windows were down and lights were off with only the television on. "Get over here," he said to me as he motioned me with his hand. I was standing outside the doorway when he said that so I took a step. "I want to promise you something," he continued as I was now one step off the threshold. He warned me about making him wake up my baby sister as his, "Get over here," became a, "Get the fuck over here now," he angrily said to me. So, I booked it to my mother's side of the bed and smooshed up to my mother's bureau. I actually believed he couldn't get me from there. He wanted me to jump up on the bed so he could explain to me about the promise he was going to make with me, but I wouldn't. He pulled a bag up from the floor on his side of the bed and pulled a doll out of it. "You can have this," "Here just take her," he continued as he stretched his arm long enough for me to not be able to reach it. "Jump up here," he continued a few more times before giving up as I showed no interest in his promise or the doll, he was offering me.

Then he questioned me if I wanted to go out the bedroom door and leave, I answered, "Yes." Then he questioned me again and again I answered, "Yes." He questioned me again and again and again until my answer became just a nod of my pouting face. Then he gave in, "You can go," he said to me as I looked at him to make sure he said what I heard him say. "Go ahead, you can go," he said again and I made a dash for the bedroom door. But just as I reached the doorway of his bedroom he was already off of his side of the bed, blocking me from running out of the doorway as he closed the door. He lifted me up and carried me to my mother's side of their bed where he laid me down. He continued to warn me about the trouble I would be in if I woke my baby sister up as he continued to explain, "I only want to make a promise." In order to do that, he insisted I had to stop crying. The more I tried to get away, get off the bed and away from him, his strength was just too overpowering.

A Childhood Tragedy Under a Mother's Watch

After what seemed like forever, Dave became impatient with me and put his legs around me. "It's called a scissors hold," he told me. I continued to try and get out of the hold he had me in as I cried and cried until he grabbed me by my jaw, squeezing as he told me with his clenched teeth, "Stop fucking crying," "I need to explain my fucking promise to you," he continued to remind me, telling me there was no way I could squeeze through the hold he had on me while laughing at me for thinking I could. I finally stopped crying and trying to get away from him but only because I was tired out from crying and trying to get away from him.

He was so happy when I calmed down. Hysterically laughing at me for a few minutes, he changed from being a scary, mean man laughing to a scary man who was now crying. He had tears in his eyes as he explained that God told him if he got me to do a promise, then God said he wouldn't have to hurt me anymore. "You want me to stop hurting you, right?" he questioned me with a sadness on his face as he explained that if I didn't do this promise then God was taking him away from my baby sister. "She's the only one who has a dad," "Want her to grow up and know you killed her father?" he continued to question, explain and cry about this promise God told him to keep with me. "All you have to do is," he said as he explained that without crying, without being forced, all I had to do was touch his penis. I didn't want to but I had no choice. It was either touch his penis or God was taking him away and everyone will blame me, hate me and not want me in the family anymore. So, I touched it. Even though we were inches apart as he continued to hold me in the scissors hold, it seemed like there were miles between us as my tiny arm stretched to touch his penis. Then I tried to jump out from his hold but I couldn't. "There's one more thing you have to do," Dave continued to say, "You have to kiss it," he said to me as I started to cry more. After what seemed like another period of forever, I had no choice but to stop crying and kiss his penis. So, I kissed it. "See that wasn't so bad," he said to me as he made me lay in his bed on my mother's side while he watched television. I just stared at the bedroom door waiting for my mother to come home from work.

Finally, my mother came home and I was still laying in the bed. She yelled at me, "What the heck are you doing up?" "Get to bed," she continued as soon as she opened her bedroom door. I jumped off the bed and ran out the bedroom like I wanted to hours earlier. Shortly afterwards, my mother came into my room asking me, "Why were you in my bed?" Like every attack before, I told my mother everything. "He made me mom," "He made me touch and kiss his pee so he could promise not to hurt me anymore," I said to my mother as I cried in my bed to her about Dave. Suddenly her loving kindness kicked in as her eyebrows raised and a smile went on her face. "He promised you that?" she questioned me. I looked at my mother a bit confused as I answered her question with a slow motion yes. Then my loving mother said with a smile on her face, "Good," as she walked away and out of my bedroom. I'm not sure if she said, "Get to sleep," or "Get some sleep," as she walked out because I was still wondering why she said, "Good."

The confusion that went through my head that night. I was glad he wasn't going to hurt me anymore but I was confused as to why, with all I said to my mother about the promise Dave made me do, all my mother got out of it was, "He promised you that," and, "Good." I approached my mother the next morning about what he made me do to make the promise. But like so many times before, her hands went up in the air as she yelled, "Jesus Christ," as she would shoo me away. I continued to take the bus to school where I was a very quiet kid. I continued to play with the girl next door, play on the front steps, backyard, playroom in the attic and my room. All without worrying about being attacked, because Dave promised he wouldn't anymore and I believed him.

Dave was taking us all for rides again to look for a camper he wanted to buy. Sometimes going for long rides to places that sold campers while my mother was at work. One night we came home to see the police outside the house. My mother came home from work and we weren't home so she called the police. I wanted to run back outside to the police officer after we were quickly escorted inside the house. But I wasn't sure if it was the same police that Dave knew, as it was one of his many threats, he told me to keep me quiet. So, I just sat on the inside stairs remembering the promise he made to me and how he has kept his promise. So, I said nothing to the policemen outside. My mother came inside the house and caught me sitting on the stairs. I was supposed to be getting ready for bed. She yelled at me, "What are you doing?" The brat in me shouted, "I should tell them about your boyfriend." Just as he walked in the front door from being outside talking to the officers. Boy did he shoot me a dirty look as I jumped up from the stairs and went into my room where life continued on.

Soon it was my ninth birthday, December 1978. I was used to not having a birthday party. I got a cake, a present from my mother still in the store bag and happy birthday being sung by my brothers, mother and her boyfriend. It was shortly after my birthday but before Christmas when I learned the hard way, just what happens when someone you make a promise with has their fingers crossed behind their back.

I was in the living room with my brothers and our baby sister was sleeping upstairs in her playpen. Dave came into the living room asking for my help to wrap my mother's Christmas gifts he said Santa just delivered to him. It was the first time since knowing Dave that I felt no fear or so I thought. A few months had gone by since he made the promise to me and he kept his promise since. I jumped up at his offer to wrap Christmas gifts. He escorted me upstairs and gave me everything I needed to wrap a bathrobe for my mother. My sister was still awake and poking her face into the netting of the playpen and making me laugh. I continued to play with my sister through the playpen when Dave went into the closet to get another gift for me to wrap. But he came out saying there were no more gifts to wrap as he informed me, "Santa Clause would finish the rest."

He then kneeled down next to me and put his hand on my shoulder asking if I remembered the promise we made. I told him I did and even reminded him of it, "You promised me you wouldn't hurt me anymore," I said to him. He agreed with me as he sat down on his bed, holding my hand and positioning me to stand in front of him, facing him as he continued talking to me. He was so glad I remembered the promise. He said it meant, "You're listening to me." He held me by my two tiny hands with one of his and kept his other hand behind his back. He started to explain to me with a smile on his face and happiness in his manner as he told me, "A story about promises broken," he giggled. I think I caught on instantly as I kept trying to free my hands from his hand. I tried pulling away the more he talked about how I am supposed to make sure when I make a promise that the person doesn't have a hand behind their back with crossed fingers because then the promise didn't count.

As he explained to me how some people put a hand behind their backs and cross their fingers when they make a promise, I looked at him and noticed he had one hand holding me and his other hand with crossed fingers. Realizing what he was saying, the fear I once felt was instantly back. He teased me that I should have checked to see if his fingers were crossed behind his back when we made the promise. I started to cry as I pleaded, "No, no." He shook his head up and down as he said, "Yes." I tried to step back but he held onto me so I couldn't. I pleaded, "No, no," as I cried. His whole arm came over me, I went upside down and landed flat on my belly, laying on the floor of my mother's bedroom. I was now looking at the bottom of my baby sister's playpen as I continued to hear Dave laugh about broken promises. My jaw hurt but my fear of Dave was deeper. I was afraid to jump up and run, yet I was afraid to just lay where I landed on the floor.

He quickly began licking my face, holding me down and preventing me from getting up by sitting on me or kneeling his knee into my back. He let me cry, kick and squirm to get free as he laughed at me the whole time. Insulting me, flicking my head until I stopped crying. Laughing at me for crying and insisting I stop at the same time. He then sat down in front of me, cracked opened a beer, lit a cigarette and proceeded to tell me, "I'm only teaching you a lesson," as he laughed while he talked, "You can't trust no one." An excuse he used for not keeping his promise. He finished his cigarette, his beer, he got up and covered my baby sister's playpen with a blanket. I watched him as he did that. When suddenly he lifted my head from behind, placed a piece of duct tape over my mouth and pressed my head back down to the floor. With his teeth clenched he said, "Cathy this is how it's going to be." It was all I heard as I laid on the floor and saw the top of a white cloth going over my face pressing hard until I fell asleep.

A Childhood Tragedy Under a Mother's Watch

My eyes opened when I saw my mother standing at the doorway of my bedroom, she was just standing there. I could hear the creaking of the hallway floor as she stepped over the threshold of my doorway and closer into my bedroom. She saw my eyes open and questioned me, "Why are you already in bed?" As she explained it was school vacation and it was ok if I stayed up later. I told her that I was in her room and how Dave tricked me and he crossed his fingers when he made that promise. I started crying so my mother sat down on my bed. She questioned me about what he said and what he did. I told her it all, about the white cloth that made me fall asleep and how I was now in my bed. I told her, "He tricked me," and, "He broke his promise," as I cried and continued telling her about Dave holding me down on the floor, licking my face, covering my baby sister's playpen with a blanket. I told my mother, "He put me here," as I referred to why I was already in my bed. My mother sat on my bed, I cried and once again I told her everything. It wasn't until I was done speaking when my mother finally responded to all I said to her regarding what Dave did to me that night. I don't know if she hugged me or if I hugged into her but she said to me, "You know Santa is coming in a few days, right?" Was the first thing out of her mouth and then she explained Santa was coming in just a few days and questioned if I wanted to ruin everyone's Christmas, that it would be my fault if Christmas got ruined. "You don't want to ruin Christmas for everyone else, do you?" Another round of motherly love from my mother to her nine-year-old daughter.

My mother then continued to explain to me the trouble that I would cause if she called the cops on Dave. "He would be hauled to jail," "You kid's would all be split up," "Santa wouldn't know where to bring your gifts," "It will be all your fault if Christmas got ruined," as she reassured me that she, "Would talk to Dave." Telling me to worry about what I wanted Santa to bring me in just a few short days. On Christmas morning, my older brothers and I were allowed to grab our stockings that hung on the stairway wall as you walked up the stairs to our bedroom's. We got our stockings and back to our rooms until our mother said it was ok to go downstairs and open gifts. This Christmas morning before I could go downstairs, my mother made me go into her bedroom so Dave could have a talk with me. I didn't want to and threw a little fit because I just wanted to go downstairs to see what Santa left under the tree. But I was only nine years old and had no choice but to do what I was told. When my mother walked me into her bedroom, Dave was just walking out of their closet when my mother said, "I told her you just want to talk." Dave agreed all he wanted was to talk to me.

As he watched my mother walk down the stairs he quickly turned around, grabbed me by the bottom of my jaw and held me in a tight grip. "I told you to keep your fucking mouth shut," he said with his teeth clenched. "Didn't I?" he angrily continued. I shook my head yes, as he wiped my face of the tears I was crying. "Let's go open some gifts." he continued to say as I was escorted downstairs to open my presents. Christmas day at my mother's was spent opening our gifts, playing with our new toys and either staying home or going for a visit to my Aunt Jackie's house. My mother would put a turkey in the oven and have Dave watch over it, as he still never came for any of the visit's we would take with our mother to her friend's or sister's homes.

Sometime during the week of Christmas school vacation, I walked into the kitchen as my mother was complaining of our vacation being interrupted and informing us that we all had to go for a ride. "Because of your grandmother," my mother snapped at me as she went on about my grandmother being a pain and hounding her to see me. My older brothers weren't bothered about going for a visit to my grandmother's. I think the only one bothered by it was the one who bitched about it the whole ride there and made it clear, "We are not staying long," my mother sternly said. My grandmother had gifts for me and my brothers but didn't know about my baby sister being born. My mother didn't stay long at my grandmother's house, as my grandmother spoke her mind and my mother did her thing when she didn't want to hear you, she walked away.

Now 1979 and it was back to school, playing in the attic playroom, reading a book from the RIF book bus, doing a latch hook kit and dodging Dave any chance I could. He would come into my room minutes after my mother left for work. I would huddle to the corner of my bed and try my hardest to push myself through the wall just so he didn't get me, but he always did. If my brothers were out in the hallway, he would warn me about talking before escorting me to his room pretending to be playing while giving me a noogie on my head. If my brothers weren't home, he would put me in poses in the bathroom and take photos of me, getting angrier the more I cried, moved or tried to get away and sometimes, he would just use the cloth over my mouth and nose. He would threaten me of coming home to find my family dead or him being friends with the principal at my school, police officer's and how he has people watching me. My mother would complain I was complaining too much, she would get disgusted in me, walk away from me, totally ignore me, shoo me away and yell, "Go play." I was nine years old and I was feared into silence by Dave and shamed into silence by my own mother.

One day my mother was on the phone crying hysterically and yelling to whoever was on the other end of the phone. When she slammed the phone down, I questioned her what was wrong but she snapped at me to get out of her way. I moved out of her way and stood to the side as I was curious to know why she was crying. I think I knew it involved my baby sister as my mother was holding her, lifting her arm up and crying at what she was seeing under my baby sister's arm. A lump was noticed under her arm and my mother would spend the day on the phone crying to doctors about it, hanging the phone up, calling another doctor or hospital or whoever would listen to her screaming. Soon Dave came home to take my mother and baby sister to the hospital to be checked out. I was left home with my brothers where we just hung around the house as we waited to hear about our sister. Around dinner time Dave came home with a pizza for us to eat and informed us that our mother and baby sister would be staying overnight at the hospital. Soon it was bedtime, pajamas, brush teeth and bed. I guess I thought with all that was going on with my baby sister, Dave wouldn't hurt me and I believe that's what I fell asleep thinking about, Dave not hurting me or my baby sister.

"Shhh," "Shhhh, it's only me," I kept hearing as I started to kick my legs and try to get out of his arms. It was Dave, he came into my room while I was sleeping and carried me into his room, laying me down on my mother's side of the bed. "You get to play my wife," he said to me before walking back to the bedroom door and closing it. "Only until your mom comes back," he continued talking as he jumped onto the bed. I jumped up in an attempt to jump off the bed but he prevented me from doing so. I cried then I screamed and just as quickly he slapped his hand over my mouth, grabbed the back of my head with his other hand and warned me about waking my brothers up. He kept telling me over and over again to stop crying. Occasionally flicking me in my head until he stood up with his back towards me and turning around with a cloth he shoved in my face. When I woke up, I was only in underwear. The room was lighter even with the shades down as the sun peeked through the side of the shade in each window. Realizing where I was, I knew I didn't want to be there. I quickly jumped out from the blankets that covered me, jumped off the bed as I made a quick run for the bedroom door, but I was stopped. I didn't even see Dave in the room, but he was there and he prevented me from leaving. Dave quickly escorted me away from the bedroom door as he walked me towards his side of the bed. He made me stand still in the middle of the floor as he told me about the trouble, I caused him by trying to escape from the bedroom.

"You blew all chances," he yelled into my face as he continued, "I'm not going to be a nice guy anymore." He kept saying it was my fault as to why he was so mad. He continued giving me a speech about why he was being mean to me, only stopping to say, "Shut up," or, "Stop crying." Then he grabbed me by my head, lifting me off the floor until my face was leveled with his evil angered face as he ordered me with his teeth clenched, "Shut the fuck up and listen," he hollered. Placing me back onto the floor, holding me by my shoulder with one hand and pulling his penis out of his underwear, demanding I touch it, hold it or kiss it. After hearing my brothers on the other side of his closed bedroom door, he kneeled down to me and angrily questioned if I wanted my brothers to die? "I will kill them right outside the door," he warned me. I was crying and shaking my head

A Childhood Tragedy Under a Mother's Watch

no as he rubbed my head telling me to be quiet so he could go tend to my brothers. Dave came back into his room with a bowl of cereal and a banana for me to eat. Walking me to the bathroom when I had to go and still not letting me put on clothes. When I tried to go into my room to get some clothes, he stopped me and directed me back to his room. He gave me a lesson on how to eat a banana properly as he shoved it into my mouth and told me how lucky I was to be laying in my mother's side of the bed. As the day went on, I didn't stop crying. Dave would leave the room a few times to tend to my brothers and give me time to stop crying as it caused him to get more angrier the more, I cried. He spent the day keeping the shades to the windows in the bedroom closed and forcing me into positions so he could take pictures with his polaroid camera. Displaying the pictures across my mother's bureau as they developed.

When I didn't stop my crying, he became aggravated and grabbed me by my arm, threw me inside the bedroom closet like I was a bowling ball and slammed the door shut. It was cold and dark inside the closet with a sheet of thick plastic covering the window to keep the cold draft from coming in but failing to do so. I laid down on the floor, crying and trying to stay warm until I fell back to sleep. I was soon awoken to the sound of my mother's voice. I tried opening the closet door but it was locked on the other side, so I placed my ear to the door when suddenly it opened. The room was brighter than when I first woke up earlier and there was my mother standing at the opened closet doorway as I quickly wrapped my arms around one of her legs. Just as quickly she moved me out of her way and yelled at me for being in her closet. "What the heck are you doing in here?" "Go put on some clothes," she continued yelling and rushing around her closet and bedroom while I tried explaining to her why I was in her closet. "Mom he put me there," I said as I was once again crying and telling my mother what Dave did. "He wanted me to touch his pee again," I yelled as Dave stood in the room helping my mother rush to gather thing's. I guess I assumed I was getting him in trouble by telling on him with him standing right there. "Your sisters in the hospital, you think I want to hear your stupid stories?" my mother snapped at me as she rushed me out of her bedroom. Telling me again to go put clothes on. I was so confused as I went to my room and got dressed. I went to the bathroom where I washed my face of the tears and mucus from my nose. Then I stood at my bedroom doorway listening to my mother and Dave talk about my baby sister and the lump under her arm.

I watched as they rushed out their bedroom door. "Behave while I'm gone," my mother snapped at me as she quickly went down the stairs. Dave was behind her carrying a suitcase my mother had packed. He placed the suitcase at the top of the stairs and walked over to me. He escorted me back into my room so I was now standing next to my bed. He grabbed my jaw loosely as he lifted my head. "I will slice your brothers throat if you tell them anything," "You understand?" he continued in an angered evil manner. I shook my head yes and then said, "Yes." When he insisted, "I can't hear you."

I stayed home all day with my brothers just being what we were supposed to be, kid's. When Dave came home that night, he informed us that our baby sister would be staying longer at the hospital and our mother would be staying there with her. He sent us all to bed at bedtime only to carry me to his bed in the middle of the night like he did the night before. He once again placed me on my mother's side of the bed assuring me that I could go back to sleep. I once again awoke only in my underwear, I once again tried to run out of the bedroom and once again I was prevented from doing so, as he once again blocked me from getting out of the room. He told me while my mother was at the hospital it was my duty to play her role of mom. "Only until she comes back," he continued to reassure me that it was ok to play her role.

We heard voices on the other side of the bedroom door and I got excited knowing it was my brothers as my head, eyes and ears where on nothing else but that bedroom door. Dave headed towards his bedroom door when he suddenly turned back around, charged at me, grabbed my head as he angrily questioned me, "Want me to kill your brothers right now?" and he continued, "I'll put a knife right in their heart," "Want me to, huh, huh," "Huh?" he frightened an already terrified kid. I shook my head no as

A Childhood Tragedy Under a Mother's Watch

I answered him that I didn't want my brothers to die. He made me promise not to make a sound so he could go tend to my brothers. Telling me, "I'll be right back." "Your brothers are alive because of you," he said in a bit of gratitude as he praised himself on being a good stepfather, giggling as he walked out the door and closing it behind him. He came back into his bedroom and I was still sitting in the same spot and same position. I didn't move an inch when he left the room to help my brothers with breakfast because I was scared to move.

As the day went on, I didn't stop crying. He would leave the room a few times to tend to my brothers. Giving me time to stop crying as he became more frustrated the more, I cried. He spent the day keeping the shades to the windows in the bedroom closed again and forced me into positions so he could take pictures with his polaroid camera. Displaying the pictures across my mother's bureau as they developed. He continued to threaten me, "You better stop crying." Each and every time he left the room to go check on my brothers, he warned me. "You better be done crying by the time I get back," he angrily demanded. By dinner time that day the photos he took would be laid across my mother's bureau, Dave's bureau, nightstands, bed and the chair he and my mother had inside their bedroom.

He continued his lessons on how to eat a banana properly as he showed me in a sexual way of shoving the banana down my throat. "It'll help stretch your mouth," he said laughing. "Cause I'm sick of your fucking teeth," he would switch from giggling, evil and laughing and to being angry, evil and terrorizing as the torture of my nine-year-old self was only becoming eviler with every passing hour. The light from the cracks in the shades of the windows started to fade, making the bedroom darker while night time came to be. Dave became all happy and giggly as he proclaimed, "It's time to play your mother's role," as he laid me back onto my mother's side of the bed. He happily talked of how privileged I should feel for being chosen for this. He continued talking as he climbed on top of his bed, crawling up it until he was kneeled on his knees right over me. I wiggled my head, moved whatever arm or leg I could and I wouldn't keep still. Making Dave become angrier. Causing him to sit up, grab me and yell, "You been nothing but trouble since Fletcher Street." As he sent a smack upside my head causing me to now be on his side of the bed with my feet dangling off the side.

Hyperventilating as I gasped for breaths all while I was hurting and trying to stop crying like he wanted me to. He placed a fat strip of grey tape over my mouth and I watched his face go evil as he said, "Now shut the fuck up." Then he would lick my face, telling me how pretty I was and how much fun we were going to have. My hair was all over my face, tape over my mouth, tears, mucus and I was so damn scared. I wondered where my brothers were. I knew they were home; didn't they hear my screams and cries? As Dave repeatedly told me, "They don't care about you."

I was afraid to move but he ordered me to, "Sit the fuck up," he said in a stern voice while he walked around his room collecting the photos, he took of me earlier. I didn't want to make him mad again, so I turned myself around and sat up on his side of the bed. He ordered me to look at him as I kept looking at the floor or the windows straight ahead. Then he ordered me to repeat thing's he would say, "I'm worthless," or, "I'm stupid," he repeatedly had me say. Or he'd be all about himself and make me repeat, "I'm your trophy," or, "You're my master." After what seemed like forever, Dave continued going on about me being a crybaby and finally questioned me, "Do you want to go play?" I figured if I answered him the right way the first time then he wouldn't ask me again so I answered him immediately, "Yes please." But he taunted me as he made me say it over and over again. I sat there pouting, my head down, my feet dangling off the bed above the floor as I cried and answered him every time he questioned, "Do you want to go play?" I answered him every time, "Yes please." At one point I was about to jump off the bed but at the same time I also hesitated in fear of what he was up to.

He then sat down on a metal folding chair he had in his room. He drank a beer, smoked a cigarette and continued laughing at me. He also had a cooler resting on the floor next to where he was sitting. Inside were more cans of beer and ice keeping his beer cold. He continued to stare at me, yelling at me anytime I looked away, "Will you fucking look at me." Then he would casually take a drink of his beer or drag of his cigarette as if he was some kind of superstar before crushing his beer can with one hand as he stood up and said, "You know what?" he questioned as he charged at me while I tried to huddle against the wall. He grabbed me by my neck and head as he angrily told me of all the hard times, I gave him. Reminding me of calling him out when my mother came home the day before and threatening me of my brothers, my sister and my mother being killed if I didn't learn to shut up. I was crying more, screaming, "No please, no," I begged him. But he put a cloth over my mouth because he was sick of hearing me cry. I tried to wiggle my head but I was no match to his strength. Last thing I heard him say was, "This is how it's done?" when a cloth went over my nose.

I awoke in the closet with the covered plastic window. It was cold and I was hurting. My eyes were puffy from days of bawling my eyes out. The closet had boxes on the floor along one wall, shoes along the other side and clothes hanging on hangers. One side were my mother's clothes and the other side was Dave's. I grabbed one of my mother's pieces of clothing and used it as a blanket as I was still just in my underwear.

I tried opening the door but it was locked on the other side. I yelled but I was afraid he'd kill my brothers if they heard me scream, so I stopped yelling. I was so scared and confused. I wanted to be with my brothers and I just wanted my mother home. The door finally opened and I jumped right up ready to charge out the door, but I was stopped and blocked by Dave who stood in the way and prevented me from leaving. "Sit the fuck back down," he said as he pushed me with his leg while walking into the closet. "Here's some food," he said to me. "You have to eat it here," he continued. "You want to know why?" he questioned as he placed a bowl of Spaghetti O's and a cup of Kool-Aid on the floor next to me. "Because no one trusts you." he screamed into my face. Then he gave me a long stare before saying, "That's why."

I started crying but I couldn't do anything but eat because I was starving. He rushed me to finish so he could walk me to the bathroom. He wouldn't let me shut the bathroom door. "Can't trust you," he repeated saying until I walked out of the bathroom. He escorted me to his room and back into the closet, then closed the door and locked it with me inside. Hours and hours went by. I don't know where my older brothers were, I don't know where Dave went, but I did know where I was, locked inside my mother's bedroom closet. I was cold, I cried and I was scared. At one point I fell asleep only to wake up and wait and wait for the door to open. But it remained closed and not one sound could be heard except for my crying and sobbing.

After hours of no noise, nothing inside or outside besides cars that drove down the street, I heard some voices coming from outside. I squished my face up against the plastic covered window but all I could see was a blur. The thick plastic over the window made looking through it difficult. I moved the shade on the window but only saw blurry brightness. I sat back down until I heard the voices again and thought it was my brothers. I jumped up and smashed my face to the plastic, banging with my hands as I saw blurry images of people outside. I looked around the closet to find something I could break the plastic with. I used my mother's shoe to try and poke a hole through the plastic but it didn't work.

I got another shoe and another shoe until finally crying and giving up. Then I heard the voices again, I squished my face against the plastic again and I looked around the closet again. I tried using a crutch from a pair of crutches my mother had in her closet but that didn't work either. Then I saw Dave's belts, the white one he used to whack me with wasn't there because he kept that one in his dresser drawer. But he had a couple of brown, black and Indian made belts hanging in the closet. I grabbed one and used the hook on the latch of the belt to poke a hole into the plastic on the window and it worked. Then I squeezed one of my tiny fingers into the little hole I poked into the plastic in an attempt to make it a bigger hole. As quickly as I poked my finger in the plastic, I was grabbed. Tossed like a ragdoll as I landed on the floor across the room from the closet, I was just in.

I didn't know what happened as it went so fast. I landed hard on the floor as I felt the burning sensation of rug burns on my legs and elbows. It wasn't until after I landed on the bedroom floor and tossed like I was a trash bag you toss in the barrels outside, that I realized it was Dave and I knew I was in a lot of trouble. He laughed and he laughed while he stood over me, holding the brown belt I used to poke the plastic window. I didn't move from the floor as I squished myself against the wall of the bedroom. He started to snap the belt so it made a loud snapping sound and then he ordered me to stand up, so I stood up. He then told me, "Fold your arms like this," as he motioned his arms across his chest in a crisscross manner. I folded my arms across my chest as he told me to. He went on saying, "You have no idea how much trouble you're in," as he wrapped the brown belt around my chest and fastened it. Then he grabbed a dog chain he had in his bureau drawer and tied it around my neck. He began calling me his puppy dog. Telling me that God was watching to make sure I behave and assuring me that next time he wasn't using the cloth on me. He placed a cover on a gallon jug of blue liquid, placing it and a white cloth on the floor near his bed. The more I cried, the more he yelled at me to stop crying as he yanked the belt or the chain around my neck.

He kept calling me a puppy dog. "Not even a cute one," he said as he looked at me with evil in his eyes and disgust in his face. "Do you want your sister to die?" he questioned me as he continued talking and not waiting for me to answer. "This is what God wants," he yelled as he spoke. All while laughing and praising himself. "I'm always right," he screamed in my face as he bounced up and down, all excited about the fun we were having. "This is so much fun," he proclaimed so happily and quickly changing his demeanor as he grabbed me by the back of my head, warning me that he wasn't going to be nice anymore. He agreed to take the belt off me but first I had to bark. "Like the dog you are," he laughingly said. I cried more as he continued to taunt me, "Bark," "I'll let you go," "No I won't," "Come on bark," he continued saying as he slowly pulled at the belt. Yanking it harder and harder causing me to choke. I was crying but I did bark and of course he made me do it again and again and again. He kept checking outside the bedroom door, squeezing my cheeks and jaw with one hand while reminding me to keep my mouth shut. He did it a couple of times, opened his bedroom door, looked in the hallway, shut the door and yelled at me to stop crying. "Uuuurgh shut up, will you already," he hollered.

He poked me on my forehead and on the top of my head as he yelled, "Get it through your thick fucking skull." He reminded me numerous times how no one would believe me if I told on him. Reminding me countless times about the little girl who wouldn't shut up and ended up in a trash bag. He reminded me that no one in my house would help me. He reminded me how stupid my mother was. He reminded me he had friends at my school, at the police station, in the neighborhood and how all the street poles had cameras on them. He reminded me he would know if I told anyone. He then used the cloth over my mouth to put me asleep and I awoke on top of his and my mother's bed.

Every time I awoke, he kept putting me back to sleep using the cloth. I would awake to see him playing with a camcorder that rested on a tripod, I would awake sitting between his legs as he talked into the camcorder, I would awake to see dozen more polaroid photos developing throughout the room.

I then heard a knock on the bedroom door, I heard it before and Dave would open the door and quickly close it. This time I knew the knock was one or both of my older brothers. Dave went to the door, opened it, talked for a second and closed the door. He knew it drew attention to me, "What, you think they're going to help you?" he questioned as he laughed. After a few minutes, he grabbed his polaroid camera, escorted me out of his bedroom while I was still wearing only my underwear. We walked to the bathroom where he made me remove my underwear. He filled the tub up with bubbles and he ordered me to pose in various positions while he took more photos. He ordered me to shave my legs with my mother's razor saying it would help me mature quicker so I could grow hair on my legs. He claimed he was helping me into puberty because I was still too small where I pee and he was still having trouble getting inside me. When he was done, he let me know how lucky I was to belong to him as he wrapped a towel around me.

My legs were hurting, stinging and bleeding as he made me walk out of the bathroom. He laid me on my mother's side of the bed, walked to his bureau and opened his bureau drawer. He then turned around with that brown plastic cigar tube he had given me so many times in the past. He grabbed my feet and separated my legs, trying to force the cigar tube inside me as I squirmed to get away. I screamed, "No," as I cried, squirmed and tried my hardest to not let him hurt me again. "It's your fault," he shouted while struggling to hold me still and keeping my legs separated. I was determined to not let him touch me. I continued to squirm and shake my head as hard as I could in every direction. I wouldn't stop moving causing him to squeeze my hips so I'd stay still. But there was always something on my body that was moving, my head, a leg that got loose, a skinny arm I wiggled out. He grabbed my throat squeezing until I laid still. I still wouldn't stop moving. He then sat me up as I felt a hard whack across my head that sent me back down onto the bed. Leaving me with ringing in my ears, a heaviness on my head and in a motionless mode. I just laid there unable to move yet feeling the lower part of my body move with everything he was doing. Hearing him speak as he praised himself about the, "Progress we were making." All I could do was cry as I felt pain with every touch of his hands. Keeping my eyes closed and waiting for him to stop. He kissed, rubbed and used the plastic brown cigar tube on my private area. When he was done, I curled myself up in a ball and cried myself to sleep.

I was awoken in the early morning hours when Dave carried me out of his bed and back into my bed. "Your mother and sister are coming home today," he said to me. As he carried me into my bed, he reminded me what would happen if I told anyone again. The night light was still on in the hall and my brothers were still asleep in their bedroom's. He placed me in my bed, "Go back to sleep it's still early," he said to me before walking out of my bedroom and shutting my bedroom door.

As soon as my bedroom door shut, I sat up in my bed, moved my pillow and squished myself against the wall. I sat with my arms wrapped around my folded legs as I cried and cried and cried. My legs hurt, my pee area burned, my stomach hurt, my neck burned and my head pounded. I felt shamed, I felt worthless, I felt a pain no writing, no pill, no drink, no drug and no love song could ever cure, heal, make me forget or explain. There was a quietness in the house and I was going to tell my mother everything once she got home. I thought to myself, 'Is it possible a kid can cry this many tears?' And answering my own question, 'Yes, it is.' I cried a lot that morning in my room as I sat squished against the wall, until forcing myself to get out of bed and get dressed. I put on sweatpants and crawled back into my bed still crying. I fell back to sleep, blocking everything out as I just concentrated on the tears that climbed down my nose and dripped onto my pillowcase.

I woke up to hearing a commotion outside my door, letting me know everyone was up and my mother was home. "I'm home," she yelled into my room when she opened my door just a crack like Dave does when he has me in his room and we hear a knock. "Get up," my mother continued speaking into the cracked open door. I stayed in my room and in my bed, all I wanted to do was be left alone. As the day went on, I sneaked into the hallway and into the bathroom. I sneaked back into my bedroom, shut the door and crawled back into my bed.

My mother came into my room a few times throughout the day, opening my door, telling me to, "Get out of bed," or, "Your sister's home," before quickly walking back out of my room. Each and every time I said, "Mom can I talk to you?" But she went out my bedroom door without answering. Until finally she came into my room, shutting my bedroom door and sat on my bed near my feet. "What's wrong?" she questioned me once she sat down. I sat up in my bed and told my mother about Dave locking me in their closet, the bath, her razor and what he did to me with his hands, face and brown plastic cigar tube. "Where do you come up with these ridiculous stories?" my mother questioned as she cut me off from talking. She was about to get off my bed when I yelled, "It's not a story." "I'm telling you the truth," I screamed and cried. She let me know, "You don't have to worry anymore," as she continued telling me she quit her job. "I'll be home for now on," she reassured me. Then she pretended to tickle me and question me, "Is Dave having fun with you?" I screamed at her, "It's not fun." I went on crying, telling her all about the photos and him hurting me. As I continued to cry and use the sleeve of my shirt to wipe my eyes of tears, she was gone. I yelled, "Are you kidding me?" I got out of my bed, went into the hallway and saw no one. I tiptoed down a few steps, leaned over the banister and saw my mother in the kitchen. I was so mad; I went back into my room where I tried to figure out my life.

My mother being home every night made it more difficult for Dave to drag me to the cellar, bathroom or his bedroom. So, he would attack me in my bed more than he usually did. He was waking me up with his penis in my face. Warning me of being quiet or my mother, brothers and sister would die. I always listened when he told me to shut up but I never listened when he told me to stop crying or not tell my mother. Because I always cried and I always told my mother. He continued to attack me whenever he sent my mother off to do groceries or to run errands. Punishing me more each time for telling my mother about what he does to me. He would give my mother money to run errands, leaving him enough time to drag me to his room, the bathroom or cellar and I told my mother each and every time. One morning while getting ready to run to my school bus stop, I kept staring at my mother. "What are you looking at?" she snapped at me. "Take a picture, it lasts longer," she continued. After all the commotion of three kids getting ready for school, my older brothers left ahead of me and I had a favor to ask my mother. "Can I ask you something?" I questioned her in a low voice. My mother rolled her eyes and questioned, "What now?" So, I flat out told her, "Mom he's going to kill me," "Please tell him to leave me alone," I pleaded as I began to cry. My mother got me a tissue, told me to wipe my tears, catch my bus and she would talk to Dave. "Don't worry I won't just talk to him, I'm going to tell him to leave you alone," she said to me as to reassure me that I did the right thing by telling her. I ran to my bus stop but by the time the bus got to my school, I started having second thoughts about what I told my mother that morning. It didn't take long for the thought of me going home and finding my family dead was implanted in my mind for the entire school day. It was the longest day of school I ever had.

I swore it took hours for just minutes to go by. I looked at the homeroom clock dozens of times. I would count the minutes left in the hour, watch as the clock hands moved and anxiously waited for school to end. Blaming myself for telling my mother about what Dave does to me, blaming myself for going home and finding my family dead. It would be all my fault. The bus ride home I prayed and begged God not to let him kill my family. I ran from my bus stop, down Sherman Street, onto Pleasant Street and booked it right in the front door of my home. My mother was in the kitchen doing laundry and I immediately went over to her, "Mom you don't have to say anything to him," I eagerly told her. "Please," I pleaded in desperation. "Too bad he came home for lunch," she said to me with a smirk on her face. I started to cry about him killing us all, but she laughed at me, telling me I can't go around saying that stuff. "He's a good guy," she told me as she explained I needed proof of all I say about him. "No one will ever believe you because you are just a kid," she told me in a cruel demeanor. Dave came home from work, walking into the front hallway and that's where I got my first dirty look from him that day. I knew I was in trouble for asking my mother to tell him to leave me alone. I hid behind my mother who was at the kitchen sink and when she turned around as he walked into the kitchen, I ran around her, up to my bedroom, closed my bedroom door and thought to myself, 'Stupid.' I was in trouble and I knew it. I tried avoiding Dave as much as possible, but it wasn't easy accomplishing that living under one roof.

The dirty looks from Dave continued. Screaming at night when he came into my room continued. Walking in my own home making sure I didn't cross his path continued. Screaming every time, I caught him peeking through the window in the bathroom as he looked from his bedroom side continued. My mother and Dave making comments of me being a brat, a liar and a troublemaker continued. My mother getting mad at me for not being nice to Dave continued.

One day after super I was playing in the attic playroom when my mother hollered up for me to clean up and get my snack before bed. I cleaned up and headed down the attic stairs into the second-floor hallway. As I stepped out of the attic stairway, Dave came from behind the attic door, grabbing my arm but at the same time he stepped on my foot causing me to be pulled and pushed. I went down onto the hallway floor, screaming in pain as I grabbed my leg while Dave slid me over to the stairs and shoved me, causing me to land on the second step of the stairway heading down to the first-floor hallway. My mother immediately came running up the stairs. "What the heck happened?" she questioned. I was screaming and crying in pain. Dave told her I was running and slipped. "Isn't that right, Cathy?" he questioned me as he stood over me on the top step of the stairway. I looked at my mother and just shook my head yes as I cried in pain. My mother insisted I pulled a hamstring and was taking me to the hospital. Once at St Joseph's hospital they did x-rays, gave me ginger ale, a popsicle, coloring books, crayons and kid sized crutches. I didn't pull a hamstring, I had torn ligaments in my left leg.

I had a part in an upcoming school play, something I was looking forward to be in. While at the hospital I was questioned about what happened and I told them, "My mother's boyfriend tripped me." My mother yelled at me to stop spreading lies. I was left alone in the room and when she came back in, she snapped at me about accusing Dave of tripping me. "You better knock this off or you can forget your play," she snapped at me. I was beside myself as I began to cry and she didn't have a care in the world. When the doctor came back in, I was now known as just another kid who was jealous that my father and mother were split up and my mother had a boyfriend. I was sent home on crutches and my mother yelled at me the whole ride home. She slapped me as she drove, mad that I got hurt and telling me to forget my school play if I continued with my, "Stupid stories," she said in a disgusted manner. That's what she called my cries for help, stupid stories. "Did you slip and fall?" she questioned me as she drove. I answered her with a question, "If I say that I did, will I be able to go to my school play?" My mother continued that I could go to my school play as long as I didn't say my stupid stories again. So, I told her I did slip and fall.

When I returned to school, the play was just days away and I assumed I lost my part in the play. But I didn't and I was super excited. Though I was still on crutches and unable to do the dancing part of my scene, the teacher still wanted me on stage to say my lines. Because I was on crutches, my mother had to drive me to and from school, something she wasn't happy about. When she picked me up that day, I informed her I was still in the school play. "What play?" she snapped at me as I sat in the backseat of her car. She then turned the radio up so I wasn't being heard while I answered her.

Back at home, I would wake up throughout the night to Dave slapping my face numerous times or squeezing my cheeks as he reminded me of his threats. He took my crutches from me one day and made me sit on his bed. My mother was out on an errand, my brothers were outside and I refused to open my mouth for him. He didn't have much time and I fought him too much, so he let me go. I was slowly learning by fighting more it resulted in him having less time with me. On the day of the play, I reminded my mother in the morning and she insisted she remembered. After school I reminded her again when she picked me up. I was excited to have a part in the school play of Fiddler on the Roof played by my fourth-grade class. "What play?" my mother snapped at me. "You didn't tell me anything about a play," she insisted. Once at home, she made a big issue about her night being interrupted because, "The whole world stops for Cathy," she said in a cruel demeanor. I wouldn't stop hounding her about the time. The play was held later in the evening after super time at the school. Once we were at the school, I went off with the teacher and kids in my class. My mother and one of my brother's sat in the audience. The play went on and I did my part with crutches in hand. As the play ended, everyone heard my mother's voice. She yelled, "The play was stupid and a waste of time," as she hollered my name, grabbing me by my shoulders and ordering me, "Let's go." I was so embarrassed.

I was only nine years old and already been through hell hundreds of times. I didn't know what fear was but I knew I was scared. I didn't know what shame was but I knew I was embarrassed. I didn't know what pain was but I knew I hurt. I didn't know what rape was but I knew I didn't want Dave to molest me anymore, as my mother called it. As I healed from my torn ligaments, Dave continued to send my mother out to bingo, groceries or other errands. He continued to take my crutches away from me and laugh as he'd say, "If you run then I'll let you go." Knowing I was unable to run, he'd laugh more.

Both he and my mother continued to insult, criticize and belittle me with every passing day in regards to my attitude towards the man who had been raping, abusing and terrorizing me for the past four years of my childhood. I felt so low, worthless, unloved and unwanted. Soon it was warmer weather, drives up to Fort hill and trips to look for a camper to buy resumed. My mother was still not working so she would now come with us all for the ride to Fort hill park. When we would get home she would remind me, "He didn't hurt you up there, did he?" she would question with a smirk on her face. I would give her a strange look and tell her, "That's because you were there." As out of the blue my mother would bring up me telling her about Dave attacking me at Fort hill park the year before. Because he didn't assault me when she was there, then in her eyes I was nothing but a liar.

I was about to head down the stairs one day as I came out of my bedroom when Dave stopped me before I could reach the top step. "I just want to talk to you," he said as he grabbed me by my arm and escorted me into his bedroom. He picked me up and placed me on the foot of his bed. He opened a beer, smoked a cigarette and reminded me, "I just want to talk to you," all the while never taking his eyes off of me.

He made grunts, huffs and laughed as he talked and paced across his bedroom. "You think I'm stupid?" he questioned me numerous times as his voice would get louder and angrier with each word he spoke. His teeth clenched, his face red and evil as he scared an already terrified nine-year-old. "Get it through your thick fucking skull," he yelled as he poked harder with every poke from his fingers onto the side and top of my head. "No one will help you," "You belong to me," he said as he laughed. "God gave you to me," "My trophy, mine to keep, he continued to yell in my face as his spit splashed onto my face. "Unlike the girl I shut up," "Remember her?" he screamed in my ear as he continued to tell me the same story, he told me on Fletcher Street about the little girl who wouldn't shut up so he put her in a trash bag and tossed her into a field. He continued with his cruel threats and reminding me how stupid my mother was and how no one at his work, bowling league, police, my school, his family or friends would believe me if I told on him. "Want to know why?" he laughed and screamed as he questioned me. Screaming "Yahoo," as he laughed and proceeded to tell me of a girl, he knew who was found dead in a well. "Know what a well is?" he jammed at my head with his fingers as he continued telling me he was, "Never even a suspect," he screamed as if he was celebrating. Then his demeanor changed as he became caring and sensitive with me while wiping the tears off my face with his fingers and giving me a hug. He then questioned me in a perky voice with a smile that I knew was not going to be good for me, "Want to go out and play?" he questioned. I kept my head down as he lifted my head by my chin and questioned me again, "Want to go out and fucking play?" So, I told him as I shook my head, "Yes," and he then said, "What?" as he put a finger to his ear. "Yes please," I answered him.

He began to laugh in an evil way as he reminded me about the trouble I caused. His hand came over me and the room went upside down as I felt my mid body and face hit the carpet floor of his and my mother's bedroom. I was already tasting the tears and mucus running down my face and nose. I was now looking at the bottom of their closet door, feeling his heaviness on me, unable to move as I felt his hands rubbing my buttocks while separating my legs and feeling that brown plastic cigar tube being forced inside me. I could only concentrate on the tears going down my face rather than the pain he was putting me through. When he was finished, he giggled, laughed and praised about the progress he was making with me. He kicked me, dropped his spit on me and then let me get dressed. Just before letting me out of the room, he squeezed my neck, stretched my jaw, bent my hand backwards and choked me numerous times while he made me agree to keeping his secret over and over again.

At times I felt an unbearable pain that I knew would change me forever. So many times, I left that bedroom crying and hyperventilating into the hallway as my brothers passed by me, so many times I walked right into my mother. I was learning to kick, squirm, fight and scream more as Dave continued to attack me each and every chance he could while he continued to silence me with fear. Soon we were out again looking for campers to buy so Dave could take us all camping. We drove to so many campers lots looking at pop up campers, big campers and small campers. Looking at hundreds and hundreds of campers.

I stayed by my mother's side with my baby sister or I took off exploring the lot full of campers with my brothers. As another school year came to a close in the summer of 1979, my mother would bring us to her cousin Terri's house. She had twin daughters and an above ground pool that we would go swimming in. We ate lunch at her house and made it home before Dave came home from work. Then as summer was in full swing, we packed up and went camping in Dave's new camper. We went to a few places at first, the White Mountains, campgrounds and lakes until finally staying a few weeks at Wyman's beach campground in Westford, Massachusetts. We went swimming, roasted marshmallows and we walked to the private beach which was for the campers only. We participated in the campground activities they had for kids and though I was still avoiding and staying out of the way of Dave, the fear he instilled in me only showed more and more with each passing day.

We had a campsite near the main beach and spent our days at the beach with our mother as Dave worked during the week. He left early every morning except weekends, holidays and his vacation from work. Bedtime rules were my sister first, one hour later was my bedtime then my brothers were one hour after me. My sister slept in the front of the camper and I was in the back in an area that had curtains as doors. Having a bathroom in the camper, Dave would come in pretending to use the bathroom. He would whisper my name as he stood on the other side of the curtain and poke his penis through, taunting me but unable to attack me due to the many other campers and windows being open. He was drunk one night and crawled into the back area I was in, exposing his penis from his pants. He was too drunk to get out by the time my mother came in from my screaming. She yelled at him to get back outside to the fire. Me and my mother got into an argument about me always complaining about him. Her mouth kept going as she shut the curtain to the area, I was sleeping in. She wasn't much of a loving mother and that night as I fell asleep listening to her and Dave outside laughing around the fire, I was learning to hate her as much as I hated him.

I spent most of the day time with my brothers. Walking to the campers only beach or riding our bikes around the entire campground. They had hills and trails behind the campground where horses were kept for the boys and girls club and other summer camps that visited for the day. Sometimes letting us pet the horses and take rides. There were Saturday night movies on the campers only side where we watched a movie outside the bathing house.

One day we had to pack up and go home., "We'll be back in two weeks," my mother told me as she explained we had to go home because Dave's work was having their outing at Whalom amusement park and we were going. Whalom park was a lot of fun and avoiding my mother and Dave was really easy. They hung out in the catering area that was set up for ShawPrint workers while my brothers and I were allowed to roam the park as long as we checked in with them. When it was time to eat, our names would be called over the loudspeaker. My mother would come over to me and whisper in my ear, "Was nice of Dave to let you come," "Why don't you go give him a hug or hold his hand," as she tried to convince me to go over to Dave and be grateful to him.

But I never did which caused my mother to be mad at me and she gave me dirty looks for the remainder of the day. We soon packed up again and headed back to Wyman's beach campground where the second trip was not as much fun like the first camping trip we took there. By the time our camping trip started, my mother was frustrated with the way I acted when Dave was around. She wanted me to hold his hand when we were in public, she wanted me to sit on his lap when we had a fire at night, she wanted me to go for walks with him, go swimming or play a card game with him. But I never would. I would walk away, ignore her or yell in my bratty childish voice, "Nooo." Which gave my mother a reason to ground me for yelling at her. I stepped on bees as I walked, got stung by bees as I played, drank from a soda can that gave me a fat lip because a bee was drinking from it also. My mother let me go play on the swing set that was at the public beach. But swinging wasn't fun, so I climbed the swing set. As I used the top metal bar to pull myself up, my right hand went into a hole in the top bar and right into a hornet's nest. It was painful but not as painful as what Dave would put me through. My mother would let me walk with my baby sister, giving me barriers of how far I could take her and with a public bathroom right across from our campsite, I was walking my potty-training sister over quite a bit. Even with all the bee stings and hornets swelling my hand, my mother still grounded me for not respecting Dave.

My punishment included no swimming, no camp activities, no movie at the campers only recreation area and no bike riding. All because my mother said I was disrespecting Dave. I would continue to avoid him as much as I could and my mother continued to be agitated with my behavior towards him. She came over to me numerous times telling me how much I was hurting his feelings by acting like the brat I was being. She constantly told me to go over and talk to him, then she'd get mad at me when I didn't. We would walk to the beach as a family and he would try to hold my hand. I would refuse his offer or fight to pull my hand away and my mother would get so mad at me for the insult and embarrassment I did to him in front of other people who were there camping or walking by us.

Back at the campsite, my mother was doing all she could to get me to appreciate Dave. "You're being a brat," she'd snap at me. "He's a good man," she would continue to lecture me about my behavior towards Dave. Until one day she told me I was taking a ride with him to get corn on the cob. "No," I screamed at my mother. She grabbed me by my arm and ordered me to go. "It's just down the street," she yelled at me. I looked up and there he was hearing everything I said and everything my mother was saying. I was only a kid so I had no choice but to take the quick ride down the street to get corn on the cob for dinner. I pouted as I got in his truck and then we drove away.

He talked about how much fun it was to be camping. He drove down the road to where they sold corn. He was friendly towards me as we picked out the corn on cob. He paid for the purchase and we got back into his truck to head back to the campsite. He started talking about, "Little girls who don't listen," he said as he explained while he talked of an older woman, he raped but how he liked one's my age better. "Older ones fight too much," he said to me as he laughed.

When I noticed he went past the road to Wyman's beach I yelled that he was going the wrong way. But he yelled at me, "Shut the fuck up." He explained he needed to get something at the house and we were driving there to get it, I immediately began to cry. "You know how easy it is to make you disappear?" he questioned me. He went on again telling me about the little girl he put in a trash bag because she wouldn't stop crying. He went on again telling me how no one would believe me if I told on him. He went on again telling me about the girl found dead in a water well and how he was never a suspect and he went on again telling me to, "Shut the fuck up," the more I cried.

As we pulled up to our home there were teenagers hanging outside on their porch right next door. He opened his door as I told him I would wait in his truck while he ran inside the house. He told me it was against the law to leave a kid in a truck by themselves. I had no choice but to get out of the truck. I did not want to go inside the house with him so I immediately said, "I'll wait right here," as I sat on the front steps with the teenagers close by. Dave was inside for a few minutes when I heard, "Cathy your moms on the phone." I turned around and saw Dave standing at the screen door. "There's no phones at the campsite," I said to him. "No, she's calling from the office and wants to talk to you," he continued to say. "She'll be mad if you don't see what she wants," he said in a matter-of-fact manner. So, I walked into the house and headed straight to the kitchen where the phone was. I didn't realize the phone was hung up when I picked it up from its base. "Hello," I said into the phone, but there was no one on the phone. I looked at Dave, hung up the phone and ran as fast as I could. I ran through the dining room, the living room in hopes to make it to the front door, but he got me, threw me over his shoulder and carried me to his bedroom.

He placed me down and sat me on his bed. He explained he had no time to fight with me as he pulled a white cloth from his pocket and a gallon of blue liquid from underneath his side of the bed. I cried and then I screamed just as a gust of wind came through the windows. Dave noticed the bedroom windows were left open and with the teenagers outside, he knew they probably heard my screaming. "You got lucky this time," he said to me as he put the cloth in his pants pocket, the jug of blue liquid back under his bed and escorted me down the stairs to the front door. "Go straight to the truck," he ordered me before opening the front door. I ran out, passed the teenagers outside and into his truck.

On the drive back to camp he continued to yell how ungrateful I was as he smacked me upside my head while he drove. Stopping at the gas station before the campsite so I could stop crying and clean my face up before he pulled into camp. When we got back to the campsite, I ran out of his truck crying to my mother. "We didn't just get corn on the cob," I cried to her but she just walked away from me. I went over and played with my baby sister, waiting for the right moment to tell my mother about Dave driving to the house and saying she was on the phone. My mother was a little upset about how long he took and my dirty looks caused her to come over to me a few times asking where we went. But he was always watching so I kept walking away from her. It wasn't until the next morning when I awoke and the truck Dave drove was gone. I ran out of the camper to see my mother already outside. I ran over to her, "Where is he?" I questioned her about Dave. She answered he was at work. I told her about the ride to get corn on the cob. I told her about driving home instead of driving back to camp, I told her about him saying she called from camp, I told her about the blue liquid jug he uses to put me asleep and I told her where he kept that jug of blue liquid, "Right under his side of the bed," I told her. My mother walked away but a few minutes later she came over to me with some advice. "So, we don't ruin it for everyone," she said with a smile, "Just keep what you told me between me and you," she said as she continued explaining how it would be my fault if we all had to end our camping trip early.

I guess a part of me wanted my mother to pack us all up and head home. But then that meant I would be home where Dave was always able to attack me. So, when my mother told me not to ruin everyone's summer vacation and just keep what I told her between us for the remaining stay at camp, it made sense to me. What didn't make sense to me was that for the next couple of days as our camping trip was coming to an end, my mother continued trying to convince me to hold Dave's hand when we walked through the campground. She continued trying to get me to sit on his lap around the fire. She continued trying to get me to play a card game with him. "Just so he doesn't suspect anything," she assured me. "So, he doesn't know you told me," she continued as she explained her reasons to why I should be nice to her boyfriend. But I wouldn't hold his hand, sit on his lap or play a card game with him. I avoided, stayed away from and did anything I could to not interact with Dave as I had been already doing for years.

It was finally the day to return home, we had to check out of the campsite by noontime. I was wondering to myself if Dave was going to get into trouble when we got home. But I quickly reminded myself who my mother was and realized she probably wouldn't say a thing to Dave. I became upset knowing my mother wouldn't say anything to him but I also dreaded going home because I knew Dave was always hurting me at home and at the campsite, he wasn't able to. Once at home, I was still carrying camping stuff into the house when my mother called me into her room asking me where I said he kept the jug. I walked over to Dave's side of the bed, pointed my finger and said, "Right there," as I pointed to the floor under my mother's bed. My mother got down on her hands and knees, reached under the bed before standing back up and saying, "There's nothing there." I then responded, "No, way under behind the bedpost." My mother gave me a strange look but she kneeled back down and stretched her arm underneath the bed behind the corner of the bedpost. She then pulled out a gallon jug of blue liquid, got up on her feet, told me to go inside my room and shut my bedroom door.

My mother stood at the top step as she hollered for Dave to get upstairs. My bedroom door was open a crack as I watched my mother stand at the top of the stairs with the jug of blue liquid in her hands. Then I watched as my mother started beating Dave with the jug as he came up the stairs. There was yelling, screaming and then a slam as the bedroom door to my mother and Dave's room slammed shut. There was more yelling, more screaming and then Dave came out of his bedroom with a bag packed of clothes. He headed downstairs and right out the front door.

My brothers and I heard our mother crying through her closed bedroom door so we opened it, but she yelled at us to leave her alone. She kept our baby sister in the room with her as my brothers and I did what she told us to do, we left her alone. It wasn't until the next day when we were told that our mother and Dave had split up. I don't think it fazed my brothers, my baby sister was too young to understand and I was happier than pigeons shitting on a bridge. I was super happy, I would run down the inside stairs thinking to myself, 'My mother does love me.' It wasn't easy to be a single mom of four kids in 1979. School was about to start, Halloween costumes, Christmas shopping, I'm sure it overwhelmed my mother. Not because of providing for her kids but mostly because of her image being tarnished.

My mother started a job at King's department store in Tewksbury Mass. Working nights and weekends. She would have her friend Theresa come over to babysit us kids and Theresa's kids would also come over to hang out when they weren't with their father. I was swimming in freedom, the freedom to walk around my house and not worry about Dave scooping me up, assaulting and torturing me. The freedom of going into the bathroom and not having to keep looking at the window above the shower wall in fear of seeing Dave taunting me. The freedom of knowing when I fell asleep at night, I was not going to be woken up by him.

The freedom of knowing I wasn't going to be hurt anymore, he wasn't going to touch me anymore. The freedom of knowing my mother believed me. Yes, that's the freedom I was swimming in as a nine-year-old kid. But that freedom would be short lived as one day I walked into the kitchen and saw my mother sitting at the dining room table with her head in her arms, crying hysterically. "What's wrong mom?" I questioned her. She lifted her head, gave me a dirty look, a nasty face expression and snapped at me, "You know what's wrong," "It's all your fault this happened," "You hated him ever since Fletcher Street," my mother continued to yell at me before screaming, "Get out of my face, I can't stand the look of you." I was a bit taken back by my mother's reaction to me asking her what was wrong. I guess I believed she loved me when Dave moved out, I guess I believed she finally blamed him, but nope, there she was blaming me. So, I did what she told me to do, I got out of her face. I went back outside where I thought to myself, "He's not living here anymore." I think I may have sung it to myself or hummed it as I played hopscotch. I just kept smiling knowing he wasn't living with us anymore, or so I thought.

As a nine-year-old I guess I was still seeking my mother's affection, her approval and her love. None of which she was capable of giving unless it was a show for her image, her reputation or her gain. Later in the day when I had to go inside, I quietly walked over to my mother who was in her bedroom. I told her I was sorry she was crying earlier in the day and I was sorry I got in her face as I attempted to wrap my arms around her hips to give her a hug. She quickly whipped my arms away from her. "He's been sleeping in his truck," she snapped at me. "He's a good man," she continued. Hollering at me, "You ruined everything." I just walked out of her bedroom and into my room. I sat on my bed where I thought, begged, prayed and pleaded, 'Please don't let him come back, please don't let him come back.' I said to myself hundreds of times.

My brothers and I played around Pleasant Street with the neighborhood kid's. School was back and I was back at the Oakland school again which was changing its name to the Leblanc School. We went back to catholic school classes at the Immaculate conception church and life was good, for a week or two anyway.

Autumn 1979, the crisp leaves and fallen chestnuts all along the Belvidere section of Lowell made for a fun fall season. We would take handfuls of leaves and stuff old clothes to make scarecrows or make piles so we could jump into it. I wore just as much leaves in my hair as I did barrettes. I began thinking about when my mother had two other boyfriends before Dave came along, I remember my mother smacking me when I would ask about my dad, I remember how mean my mother was towards me even before Dave came along. But I wanted my mother to love me, it wasn't fair that all the kids at school had nice mom's and my mom was so mean to me. She was my mother, she had to love me, right?

One day in early fall and just weeks after school started, I came home running from my bus stop on the corner of High and Sherman Streets. I didn't even see his truck parked outside but I did see his feet on his recliner chair as I walked into the house. It was all I needed to see. My mother was in the kitchen and I ran right to where she was. "Why is he here?" I questioned her. "Mom," I continued with a scream as she just ignored me while she was doing some cleaning at the kitchen sink. Then her face squished in disgust as she said, "Cathy don't start." I cried to my mother, "Why is he here mom?" I was so heartbroken and confused. "I asked him and he swore he never touched you," my mother said to me. "Mom you know he does," I continued to defend myself. My mother went on about how he misses us all and he was miserable without us. Telling me how she loves him and how I am too young to understand. I cried as I questioned her, "So let him keep attacking me?" My mother answered, "I believe him." I just looked at her with tears in my eyes. "So just forget about me?" I cried to her. "What about me, mom?" I pleaded to her. She continued saying he was a good man. "He provides for us," she said as she defended his actions towards me. I was about to storm away when my mother grabbed me by my arm as she leaned into me and said, "Don't go blabbing any of this to your friends," "People look down on kids who are abused," she continued. I started to bawl my eyes out as I pleaded with my mother, "It's not my fault," I cried to her. She then looked me right in my eyes and said, "To bad it already happened," "Nothing you can do about it." she insisted. When she saw I was still in disbelief she said, "You need proof, nobody will believe a kid." I ran up to my room, cried, got mad and learned to live in a house where I was slowly becoming a stranger in my own home.

Things quickly went back to the same old routine in regards to my mother and Dave's work schedule. He worked days, she worked part time nights and weekends. Dave pretty much kept his distance from me at first, he didn't taunt me, he didn't come into my room at night. But I still stayed very cautious of him. My mother was quickly back to being frustrated with my lack of effort to be nice to Dave. "He's not bothering you anymore, is he?" my mother questioned me one day as she threatened to ground me if I didn't make an effort to be nice to him.

With all that monster put me through, what he did to me, what he forced me to do, I actually thought about being nice to him. Maybe my mother would love me then? Maybe I'll be part of the family again? Maybe he'll be nice to me? Maybe my mom would be happy? Maybe we'll be a real family? Maybe he'll never touch me again? Maybe, right? I had to work up the nerve to approach Dave. I would watch him as he joked with my brothers or played with my baby sister. But I had a fear of him that was just brushed off to people in the public eye as a shy little girl. I was still wondering every night why he was back living with us. Why didn't my mother believe me anymore? Why does he make me so scared of him? Why has my body felt so different since Fletcher Street?

Soon it was getting dark early and I wasn't able to go out as much after school or when my mother worked the night shift. I was flat out scared of Dave and it wasn't long before he reminded me of that fear. One day he took us all to Fort hill and let my brothers go roam the park to play. He made me stay with my baby sister. He pulled me closer to him as he started doing what he has been doing for years, forcing me to masturbate him. I cried and cried and with other people on the hill and my brothers being close by, Dave had no choice but to let me be. He threatened me to keep my mouth shut by squeezing my hands backwards. I was afraid to tell anyone because I knew he would kill them. Anyone, my brothers, teachers, my principal, neighbors, cops, strangers, Dave would kill them all, even the people on top of the Fort Hill in the fall of 1979.

One day at home while I was going up the inside stairs, I didn't see Dave's arm come over my head, covering my face as he put me in a headlock while giving me a noogie. He escorted me into his and my mother's bedroom, he flung me onto his bed, then he shut the bedroom door. I rolled off the bed so I was standing by his side of the bed. He kept pushing me back down onto the bed, but I kept jumping off the bed. He chased me around the room saying he wasn't letting me out of the room until I calmed down and listened to what he wanted to say. He charged at me yelling "Sit down, shut up and calm down." He would pick me up, place me on the bed and I would jump back off the bed trying to get to the bedroom door, trying to get away from him. "I just want to talk to you," Dave kept saying to me, "I just want to talk to you," while he chuckled over the fun he was having by watching me as I kept trying to run by him, through him, under him or over him. I kept trying to get out of the bedroom. He let me keep fighting my way out as he blocked and prevented me from doing so until I wore myself out. I finally sat down, I stopped trying to get to the door, I stopped trying to get away from him and I sat on the foot of my mother and his bed as I listened to what he wanted to say to me. Dave started his talk with me, "You blew a good thing," he said as he giggled. He chuckled, laughed and hollered in my face," You blew a good thing." He paced back and forth across his bedroom. As he paced, he would stop quick, turn to me and yell in my face and ear, "You don't know how good you had it." Then he gave me a lecture, "This is all your fault," he went on about it being my fault because I told my mother where the blue jug was. "You're clever," he said to me as he started poking my head with his finger.

"This is what father's and daughter's do," he screamed at me as he spit at me while talking through his clenched teeth. "Get it through your thick fucking skull," he continued, poking my skull and forehead with every word he said. He told me he was being nice to me by using the cloth over my mouth because it made me not cry. Then he acted sad because he was going to have to hurt me and make me cry. He put his evil face into my face as he yelled at me, "You are worthless." He angrily poked me in my forehead harder with his finger telling me to listen. He smiled as he shook his head telling me, "You don't know how good you had it."

I wondered where my brothers were, I wondered where my mother was. I kept looking at the closed bedroom door waiting for it to open, waiting for a chance to run as fast as I could out the door but I was now frozen in fear to even try. He finally stopped pacing and turned to me with his un-

1975-1982 Lowell Massachusetts

zipped pants, pulling his penis out as he grabbed me by my head with his other hand. I squirmed out of the hold but he grabbed me by my waist and whacked me against my head with his arm or hand. It knocked me down onto the floor, staring at the bottom part of the closet door and feeling my body moving. His hands all over me, tears going down the side of my face as I tasted each one that went down my nose and dripped off my messy hair. He complained I was still too small, he laughed that it was because his penis was too big to fully go inside me without me bleeding before I was supposed to. "As all young girls do," he laughed as if he told a joke. When he was finished with me, he kicked me with his feet until I got up. I got my clothes back on as he took pride in what he had just done to me. He walked me to his bedroom door and reminded me of how my family, friends, school teachers, anyone at all, he would kill if I told anyone. I had to agree to keeping our secret or he would kill me right there in my mother's bedroom. His grip around my neck choked me as I grasped for a breath but the pain was so intense, I was unable to answer him until he loosened his grip. Leaving me to walk out into the hallway hyperventilating and crying in pain.

    Each and every time Dave let me out of his bedroom after assaulting and terrorizing me, I never walked out without puffy eyes from crying, heavy breathing from the gasp of breathes I was trying to make through the pain and shame I was walking in. He always warned me about not going into the bathroom to wash him off of me, "The lotion is good for your skin," he'd jokingly say smiling as if he is that stepfather of the year again. All I could do was cry myself to sleep and let life keep going. I awoke one morning for school and my eyes were still puffy from crying the night before. I went downstairs and just stared at my mother. She acted like I wasn't there for a bit. She was making sure my brothers were getting ready for school and trying to ignore me. But I kept moving along side of her making her attempts at ignoring me a little hard. I was hurting and exhausted from crying all night when finally my mother talked to me, "Go back to bed," she whispered. "You can't go to school looking like that," she continued and as much as I wanted to go to school, it was because of what Dave did to me the night before, why I did not go to school that day. It would not be the only day I missed school because of injuries I suffered in the hands of Dave. I was learning to be outside or over a friend's house if my mother was at work. The only thing that sucked, I was only nine years old. So when you're told to you can't go outside, there is no choice but to listen to what you're told.

There were many times my mother would come into my room after Dave assaulted me and question, "Is Dave having fun with you?" I would cry and scream to her, "It isn't fun." She had so many damn excuses for him, "Maybe he doesn't realize he's hurting you?" "You take it the wrong way," "He's trying to be nice," "Come on, where do you come up with these ridiculous stories?" always adding, "You're just a crybaby." With a guarantee no matter what was coming out of her mouth, she was just as quickly storming away in total disgust with me.

As I was getting older the attacks seemed to become more of a routine in my nine year old life. Every week night my mother worked, every Saturday morning, afternoon and sometimes unfortunately for me, when my mother worked a double. Many times Dave liked to be daring and literally wait until he knew my mother was home from work to finally open that bedroom door. I would cry, gasp for breaths and walk many times right into my mother who was coming up the stairs. There was always yelling from her, "What are you still doing up?" or, "What are you crying about now?" she would continue to yell while I was still trying to answer her first question.

I finally turned double digits in December 1979. I didn't have birthday parties, just my brothers, baby sister, my mother and Dave. Although I once remembered a birthday party at my grandmother's, by age ten and with all I had been through, that memory was long lost. My birthday at my mother's lasted the few minutes it took my family to say happy birthday to me and my birthday was over. Dave continued to fear me into silence with his threats of knowing people on the police force, the street lights having videos watching me and if my brothers, baby sister and mother were killed, it would be all my fault. For some reason I went to my mother each and every time. Later in the night on my tenth birthday Dave came into my room and I immediately started to scream. My mother was in her room, I knew she was in there and I knew she heard me. "I have a special gift for you," Dave said to me as he tried to assure me, "I'm not going to hurt you," "Don't you want your special birthday gift I got you?" he continued saying over my screams, "No, get out." I continued to yell. He grabbed me by both my hands with one of his, "Shut up and listen," he leaned into me and ordered me to obey him. My mother never came into my room, no matter how many times I screamed for her.

"You need help with this," Dave said to me as he placed the brown plastic cigar tube on my blanket in front of me. "This will help you," he continued as he placed a rubber thing on my bed. "You need to get to this," he said while he shoved the rubber thing in my face. "It's a big penis, like mine is," he laughed and chuckled as if he was giving me fatherly advice. "Mother Mary will help you," he said with a laugh as he turned the penis looking rubber thing around and it was a picture of the virgin Mary on the other side with colors of blue, white and gold. "I want you to practice," he told me as if he was talking to me like he was a coach of a soccer team. "Put it under your mattress and don't tell your mother," "You'll regret it if your mother finds out," he said to me in a stern voice as he walked out of my bedroom shaking two of his fingers in the air. I moved the sex toys by flapping my blanket in the air causing them to move to the foot of my bed. Gosh my brain was so confused.

I fell asleep on my tenth birthday wondering why, 'Why does Dave hurt me like he does? Why doesn't my mother stop him? Why do they blame me? I awoke the next morning and called my mother into my room, "Look what Dave gave your ten year old daughter for her birthday," I said to my mother as I pointed to the object's on my bed. My mother shrugged her shoulders, gave me a look of disgust and said, "Jesus Christ," as she grabbed them off my bed and walked out of my bedroom. I spent the day asking my mother numerous times if she said something to Dave? I asked her numerous times if she was going to stop him from hurting me again? I asked her numerous times to call the police, "The one's he doesn't know," I insisted. I asked her numerous times to protect me from her boyfriend. I knew I was going to be in trouble for telling my mother about the birthday gifts Dave gave me and making her take them off my bed, but a part of me hoped my mother would finally stop Dave from hurting me.

I managed to avoid Dave throughout Christmas. Maybe because of the holiday, but he didn't try to assault me. He gave me a lot of dirty looks but I'd just look away, walk away or run upstairs into my room and shut my door. I was avoiding him and keeping my distance as much as I could and I wondered if he did get in trouble from my mother. 'Maybe she made him throw those sex toys away in the garbage, maybe she yelled at him, or maybe my mother got mad at him.' I would tell myself these things, I guess in an attempt to make myself believe my mother did love me. That's a lot of maybe's for a ten year old. I was learning to hate everything about myself as the approval of my mother's love failed more with each passing day.

Dave not hurting me, never happened. My older brothers who lived in the same house never cared and I believed it was my fault why no one cared about me. Just when it couldn't get any worse for me, one day after the Christmas holiday during school vacation in December, I was heading down the stairs when Dave called my name from his bedroom. "Hey Cathy," he yelled as I just froze. He said my name loud enough I couldn't pretend to ignore him. "Come here," he said while reaching for my arm and pulling me into his bedroom. "Look what I found," he said to me in a matter of fact manner as he waved those same two sex toys my mother took off my bed just a few weeks earlier. I didn't think my mother would give them back to him, but she did. I immediately began crying nonstop tears as his face grew angrier with every word he spoke. "Fucking brat," "You're fucking stupid brat," "What the fuck did I tell you," he continued scolding me as I kept crying and eyeballing the door, thinking I could run and open it but also knowing he would stop me before I got to the door. He paced his bedroom floor, getting his kicks on terrifying a ten year old kid until he turned to me and his whole hand went over my face as he flung me backwards onto his bed. Laughing about the fun he was about to have with me as he scolded me more. Calling me names and blaming me for not being able to use to the cloth over my mouth anymore. "It's all your fault," he spoke into my face with his teeth clenching. He called me, "Stupid," then he'd pet my head like I was a dog. "But you're smart too," he said while smiling. Then switch back to being evil, "Stupid fucking brat," as he continued to scold me. He was mad I kept getting him in trouble with my mother.

He would scream while poking my head until he lifted me with both his hands, holding me by my head. "It's all your fault," he yelled louder as he slammed me down onto the bedroom floor. My head hit the floor first then my feet as they bounced from the sneakers I was wearing. Then like a rag doll, I was picked up and plopped back onto his bed. I couldn't move, I don't know why but I just laid there. Feeling everything he was doing, hearing him complaining about my sneakers being in the way of my pants coming off, complaining I was still too small for him, telling me, "We got a lot of work to do." I laid there motionless, crying and waiting for him to finish touching me, finish rubbing me, finish rubbing his penis between my bum, finish touching me down where I pee, waiting for him to finish hurting me. All I could do was cry.

When he was finished, he grabbed me and yanked me off the bed, "Get out," he ordered me. I pulled my pants up and headed to the door, his foot appeared in front of me as he made an attempt to stop the door from opening. "You going to keep your fucking mouth shut?" Dave questioned me as he grabbed me by my hair, lifting me off the floor causing me to grab his arm so I could be lifted by his arm rather than by him using my hair. I screamed in pain as he continually asked me if I was going to keep my mouth shut and I continuously answered him that I would keep the secret while begging him to let go of my hair. When I left the bedroom I went straight into my room. I cried and waited to hear him in the hallway going downstairs so I could go into the bathroom and wash myself up. When my mother came home from work, I was in my room and cracked my door open until I saw her coming up the stairs. I popped out of my room, "Mom come here," I whispered so Dave wouldn't hear me. My mother came over to me, I motioned her to come inside my room and she did. "Mom he pulled me into your bedroom again," I said to her as she stared at me with no expression on her face. I started to cry as I told her, "Mom he took off my clothes, hurt my pee and poked my head." Without a word said, she walked right out of my bedroom. I jumped off my bed and followed her into the hallway. "Mom," I quietly yelled to her. "Cathy don't start," she snapped at me in disgust and went into her bedroom, closing her bedroom door and leaving me standing there in the hallway. I went back in my room, I cried and I looked out my bedroom window for hours. I was a ten year old kid in 1979, our text message was a written note folded in different shapes. Our 911 was smoke signals, our internet was an encyclopedia and our world wide web was the library. I looked out my window and wondered, 'If I ran away where can I go?' I thought all I needed was a long stick with a bag tied to it, fill it with clothes and run away. But the front door had a dead bolt I was unable to open so I just went to bed.

It wasn't long until my mother was complaining about going to a wake and funeral. "For your grandmother," she said to me as she told me, "She died." I got instantly mad at my mother as I questioned her, "Why didn't you ever take me to see her?" I was upset I hadn't seen my grandmother in awhile. Then I questioned her, "Why is she having a wake and funeral if she died?" That was when I learned what a wake and funeral was. My mother, brothers and I were going to the wake. My baby sister stayed home with Dave.

I quickly questioned my mother, "What if he does to her what he does to me?" My mother laughed at my question and answered me, "She's his blood." Dave appeared where we were standing in the front hallway as we were getting ready to leave. He pulled me by the cellar door in the kitchen, leaned down to my height level and said, "Your sister will be here when you get back." He reminded me again before we all headed out the door to go to my grandmother's wake. So many people were coming over to me calling me Catherine Alice and telling me who they were. I met cousins, brothers, a sister, step sisters and more. One man was upset that I didn't remember him and it caused a commotion as another man sat down in the chair next to me. "Do you know who I am?" he questioned me. "My real father," I answered him as I quickly stared back down to the floor I kept looking at. When my mother said it was time to leave, I got up but quickly gave a wave goodbye to the man who was sitting next to me. The funeral was the next morning and Dave reminded me again of keeping my mouth shut at the funeral. Once at the funeral home my dad approached me and hugged me causing my mother to pull me away. My dad and I kept giving each other funny faces throughout the service for my grandmother. Every time I looked over at the man I knew as my real father, he would look at me with goofy and funny faces, causing me to giggle and my mother to bend down to my level, point her finger in my face and say, "Knock it off." We were home early that morning and I questioned my mother why I didn't get to see my grandmother before she died. My mother answered by bitching about my grandmother. Telling me she never cared for me, she had other grandchildren and never liked us because she didn't like her. My grandmother didn't like my mother, that's why I didn't see her for almost a year before she died. I was mad at my mother and started to question myself in regards to my real father. Eventually asking my mother to take me to see him. She got upset that I was going to insult Dave and complained that I was being a nag to her. Then she walked away from me.

If my mother didn't want to answer a question, wanted us to do something or to get away from her, all she would do was yell, slap or raise her hand and shoo us away. I don't know if it was because I was getting older, getting taller, fighting more or just accustomed to living the life I was living under the guidance of my mother and Dave, but the attacks seemed to start lasting longer, more daring as Dave was in no fear of being told to stop, no fear of getting caught and no fear of being forced to leave me alone. No matter if I was outside playing in the backyard, front steps, in the attic, my bedroom or bathroom, if Dave wanted me, he came and got me. Forcing me to sit between his legs while we were both in just underwear as he video taped us with his camcorder. It was always set up in his bedroom on a tripod. He talked into the camera as if he was making a movie and always acted like we were having so much fun while he filmed. He took pride as he talked of how much longer I had to live. "You're mother is dumb," "You'd be dead already," he'd warn me. "Don't tell your mother and maybe I will let you live a little longer," he said as he stood me to my feet. "My trophy, " he said with pride as he stood up, then he walked over to the camcorder and I walked to my clothes. Picking them off the floor so I could get dressed, but that was not the case.

He put his hand on my shoulder, grabbed my clothes from my hands, turned me back towards the bed and said, "We're not done yet." Dave was not done with me that day and all I could do was cry. For years Dave would get mad with all the crying I did, but now he wanted me to cry. For years Dave would get angrier the more I fought and gave him a hard time, but now he wanted me to fight him and give him a hard time. For years Dave raped, tortured and terrorized my childhood and now I was getting older which caused a dilemma for him. "Do I kill you now or later?" he would start questioning me on a regular basis. I cried a lot and I was always being called all kinds of names.

I never really had a chance when it came to my mother. She had a label for me even before I knew what a label meant. I was a thief by age five for stealing snacks I didn't steal, I was a liar by age six for telling my mother about things Dave did to me or made me do, I was a troublemaker by age seven for continuing to tell my mother about things Dave did to me or made me do, I was a bad daughter and sister for always causing trouble because I didn't want to be raped or abused by Dave anymore and I was worthless by age nine, shamed and feared into a secret that would later turn into embarrassment and humiliation as I got older. So yes when it came to my mother, I had no chance at all.

I started to put together the facts in regards to my grandmother and my dad. My grandmother was my dad's mother, not Dave's. That's why my dad and uncle were at her wake and funeral. I knew who my dad and uncle were which made me remember my birthday party at my grandmother's, her stuffed animal room, her Kool-Aid and her hugs. I confronted my mother again about my dad. "Take me to my dad's," I said to her. My mother changed the subject by blaming me for, "Your stupid fucking uncle keeps calling," my mother angrily snapped at me. Instead of taking me to my dad's, she rounded everyone up to go visit my aunt and uncle. There were presents for my brothers and I when we arrived. The lady who was my aunt felt bad we were opening gifts intended for younger kids and upset the gifts had piled up throughout the years. My uncle waited outside as we had a short visit with my aunt inside. They didn't know about my baby sister so she ended up with all the toys because we were too old for them. My aunt did not like my mother, my uncle did not like my mother, but it was my mother who sensed it and caused a scene for us to leave. Seeing my uncle outside sitting on the steps, I gave him a hug before leaving with my mother.

Back at home I was meeting more kids in the neighborhood. I was learning to stay outside when my mother worked during the afternoon or Saturday mornings. I was sleeping over any friend's house I could. By the time I was ten years old, I had already walked all over Pleasant, Concord, Perry, Pond, Sherman and Porter Streets. I was making many friends and seeing classmates along the way. I was now venturing up to High, Huntington, Nesmith, Chestnut, Fort Hill Ave and Rogers Streets. I was sleeping at Tricia's on Perry St, Nani's on High St and Michelle's on the other end of Perry Street. Still not one friend ever slept at my house.

Any time I walked out my front or back door, I knew if I told anyone about Dave, I knew what the consequences were. So instead I did what was instilled in me at a young age, I went outside to go play and keep Dave's secret a secret.

As if life couldn't get anymore confusing, my mothers friend Pauline who we have been occasionally visiting throughout the years and would sometimes cut my hair at Lowell hair academy in downtown Lowell, had moved and my mother wanted us all to go visit her at her new home. My mother told me she had another baby, making it her second son. Everything seemed fine as we drove across the city to the highlands where she moved on a street that had a fire hydrant painted as a Dalmatian puppy. She was really nice and older than my brothers, but not old like my mother. The only thing a little off about this visit to my mother's friends house was the way she told us who her sons were to us, "They are your nephew's," she

A Childhood Tragedy Under a Mother's Watch

said. I could tell she was disappointed we didn't know they were our nephews. My mother had a way of disappointing people. Pauline wanted me to come over, hang out sometime and babysit. I thought it was really cool she asked me and my mother said it would be ok. I don't think I understood the whole nephew thing though. But I understood when we were leaving her house. My mother had to reverse out of Pauline's driveway. As she waited for cars to pass, my oldest brother who was in the front passenger seat started yelling at our mother, "You lie," "You're a liar," he yelled at her continuously as he pissed her off in the process. "She's not your friend," "She's your daughter," "She's our fucking sister," he continued yelling as he busted her in a lie. 'Wait, what, our sister?' I thought to myself as I was so confused.

I made many attempts to question my mother about why she didn't tell us Pauline was her daughter. Any time I attempted, my mother would quickly shoo me away, yell at me or walk away. In reality what she showed me was that she just didn't care. I continued to question, hound and throw fits until my mother finally gave in and drove me to my dad's home. I was impatiently waiting in the passenger seat of my mother's car while we drove there. As we drove up Market Street, it changed to Salem Street. Then I questioned my mother, "Where are you going?" "You passed it," I continued as my mother drove past a row of brick apartments. She then made a left turn into another row of brick apartments. "He lives there," she said to me as she pointed to a door at one of the apartments lined along the brick building. "It's not the one he lives at," I said as I got mad at my mother. We argued back and forth about whether we were in the right row of brick apartments. By the time she threatened me of driving away, I took the chance and knocked on the door my mother insisted was my dad's. A lady answered saying I was the cutest thing knocking on her door. My mother talked out her car window to the lady as if she was mother of the year for taking me out looking for my father. When I got back in my mother's car, we argued more until she said to me, "Hey at least I tried." Then she threatened to slap me if I didn't shut up. We drove back home to a place where in just one year my life would change in ways I could never imagine.

I also hounded my mother about me going over Pauline's house. I would beg, "Please mom," I begged her. "So I don't have to be home with Dave while you're at work," I pleaded with her. Chasing her down the inside stairs, out the door and to her car, I begged her from morning until the time she left for work in the afternoon. But my mother always ignored me, shunned me and walked away until finally telling me, "I called Pauline and she doesn't want you over her house anymore," she told me in a cruel manner. I questioned her, "Why not?" My mother answered me, "Because of what Dave did to you," as she proceeded to snap at me, "Told you people look down on kids who are abused." My eyes filled with tears with every word she said. But I had to know, "How did she know, mom?" I questioned her. She quickly responded, "Just look at you," "How can you not know," she said as she rolled her eyes. "Ohhhh poor crybaby Cathy always looks sad," my mother ridiculed, teased and mocked me. That's when I used the one thing I did learn from my mother, I walked away.

My mother claimed she spoke with my father. She told me he was going away on a vacation to the islands with all his other kids, step kids and, "Not you," she snapped at me as she used her lies in an attempt to shoo me away in regards to wanting to see my dad. Or maybe it was an attempt to crush what was left of my ten year old heart. Or maybe it was an attempt to just prove how nasty, cruel and selfish my mother really was to me. Or maybe it was an attempt to keep me away from seeing my father again, either way it was an attempt she won, on all the above.

There was no doubt I was afraid of Dave. He always ate his meals while he sat in the living room on his recliner chair with a folding TV tray. My mother always served him his plate as if he was a king at his throne. She made me bring his plate of food to him one day at dinner. I didn't want to, but it was a bribe my mother used on me when I asked to sleep over a friend's house. So I took the plate, walked into the front hall from the kitchen, turned to the living room and there he was, sitting in his recliner chair and his folding TV tray was set up in front of him. I stood at the doorway of the front hall and living room. One hand on the frame of the doorway, the other hand had his plate of food as I stretched myself to give him the plate. He reached forward to grab the plate from my hand, I panicked, dropped the plate, screamed and ran to my mother in the kitchen. "What the heck did you do," my mother yelled, smacked me upside my head and sent to my room with no supper. Dave continued with his way towards me, grabbing me any chance he had. If I was downstairs then he'd either carry or drag me into the cellar or up in his room. If I was upstairs then he'd carry or drag me into his room or the bathroom. He was calling me in early at night and even earlier when my mother worked on weekend nights. Anywhere I was, if he wanted me then he would come get me. Depending on how much time he had, I would be forced to masturbate him, forced to look and stare at his penis as he forced my mouth open by choking me until he was able to shove his penis in my mouth. He didn't care how much I gagged, cried and kept trying to get away. Sometimes he would be too tired, too drunk or not enough time and he would let me go.

Sometimes he would choke my neck, squeezing harder and harder for every hard time I gave him and for every time I moved after he positioned me. And sometimes it would end with that one slap that knocked my whole body into a motionless mode, making my eyes glare into tears of pain as my soul numbed to a numbness never to be the same again. I don't know why he hated me as much as he did and to hurt me as he continued to do. My cries to my mother for help were now being turned away by her frustrations of me always, "Bringing it up," she would say in disgust. The fear Dave instilled in me would only deepen with every traumatizing attack that monster continued to inflict on me. Even when my mother was home Dave was still finding ways to assault me. Coming into my room at night, grabbing me as I ran by going to the bathroom or attic playroom, forcing me to touch his penis or he would squeeze my neck, my head, cheeks and hands as he warned me again about the consequences if I told anyone about his secret. My body trembled in fear as I closed my eyes or concentrated on my tears as I waited for him to be done with me. He made jokes about how stupid my mother was numerous times as if he was saying a line from a comedy show and laughing as he spoke. Sometimes he was quick with assaulting me, he would quickly hold me behind a door that was close by, the bathroom, my room, just to keep the fear in me. He was sending my mother on errands, groceries, shopping and paying for her night out at bingo. I told my mother so many times. All the times I told her on Fletcher Street, all the times I told her on Pleasant Street and all the times I told her throughout the years. None of which protected me from Dave. His attacks were slowly becoming a game to him. Sometimes my mother would calm me down by telling me she would talk to him, but most of the time she would ignore, walk away and be disgusted with me.

Dave continued his ways with me, one night keeping me in his room with the camcorder set up on a tripod stand. He must have used the cloth on me because I was in my room sitting on the floor playing with barbie dolls and then I awoke on top of my mother's bed. Dave was in just underwear, playing with the camcorder as it rested on the tripod. He was looking through the lens of the camcorder when he raised his head above it and said, "Look who's awake." He chuckled as he reached for a cloth that was on the bed, lifted a blue jug to the cloth and shook it in a sideways motion. "We can't have that," he said as he charged at me while I laid on the bed. I rolled onto my stomach and squished my face into the bedding that made the bed. After giving him a hard time for a few minutes and not rolling over, he went on yelling about the hard times I give him. I was so scared, I prayed that he would just kill me. I was tired of all the abuse I had already endured. Then I didn't hear him anymore as the room went quiet.

The big tube television in the bedroom was on but all I heard was quietness. I laid there for a few, listening to nothing and thinking, 'he's not getting me this time,' 'he's letting me go,' and then I'd listen to quietness and think to myself, 'I'm going to get up and go straight to my room.' Then I listened to more quietness just to make sure it was safe to do so. Before I knew it, a hand grabbed a chunk of my hair and lifted my head off the bed. "Ha, you think I'm stupid?" Dave screamed in my face as he began to sexually assault me.

He made me repeat, "Please master." He made me beg, "Please stop." Over and over again. Crying my eyes out made him give me sympathy as he explained, "I'm sad too," he pouted. "But you're a smart one," he said in a perky voice. "And you have a big mouth," he continued as he laughed, telling me, "Hey I didn't plan on keeping you this long." He paced the floor more before turning to me, unzipping his green work uniform pants and shoving my face into his exposed penis. I squirmed out of his hold, but something hit my head and everything went upside down as I felt the rug burn from the carpet hit my stomach, elbow, arm, chin and side of my face. I went motionless, I felt a heaviness holding me down, I felt the tears pouring down my face, I tasted those tears as they fell. My shirt was pulled to my neck, my pants were thrown and landed between my face and the closet door I was looking at. When I saw my pants land on the floor next to me, I was already feeling the draft from my pants being off, feeling him as he praised, "I'm making progress." He would use his mouth, his hand, his penis, his brown plastic cigar tube on my body and he enjoyed every minute of it.

Something about those pants when they landed on the floor next to me, I just looked at them the whole time until he was finished. I concentrated so much on that pair of pants, I didn't know he was finished until he kicked me. "Get up and get dressed," he said. "Your mother will be home soon," he went on as he shoved me with his foot to rush up off the floor. That's exactly what I did, I rushed to get dressed and tried running right out of my mothers and Dave's bedroom door, but I didn't run fast because I was in pain and Dave stopped me in my tracks anyways. I think I might have had my hand on the doorknob when he took a hold of my neck. "You going to keep your fucking mouth shut?" Dave screamed into my face as he squeezed my throat harder and harder. "Are you going to keep your mouth shut?" "Huh, huh?" he continued as he squeezed and squeezed me by my throat. When he let go of my neck he chuckled and grabbed me by my lower jaw only to do the same. "You going to keep your fucking mouth shut," he hollered. Over and over again he continued. Over and over again, I shook my head yes as he squeezed until finally letting go of his grip on me. I fell to the floor, stood up as I was hyperventilating and hysterically crying when I opened the bedroom door. I walked out and right into my mother who was just coming up the stairs after coming home from work or bingo. "What's wrong with you?" she questioned me but my hyperventilating wouldn't let me speak as I tried to tell her, "He, he made, me, me." "Just go to your room," my mother said, "I'll be right there," she continued as she went into her bedroom. I walked by one of my brother's and straight into my bedroom. I cried, held my throat and my jaw as I gasped for breaths while I changed into pajamas. I was laying in my bed, puffy eyes and hurting an unimaginable pain when my mother came in my room and sat on my bed. "Why are you crying like that?" she questioned me. I sat up and bawled my eyes out to her. "Mom he stuck things inside me," I said as I struggled with every breath and word I said. I showed her the rug burns on my legs and neck. My mother was stone faced. She didn't even look at me, she was looking at the floor. "Mom," I yelled as I shrugged her with my arm. She got up, turned to my bedroom door and walked straight out the door. I couldn't believe my mother walked out of my bedroom.

Not a word she said, no look of pity, no look of disgust, no look of compassion, empathy or love. She just got up and walked out of my bedroom. I was like, 'Not again.' I cried and cried until I fell asleep. The next morning when I was getting up for school my mother saw my neck and she ordered me to go back up to my room to put on a turtleneck shirt. I argued with her but I was a kid being told what to do and so I went upstairs to put on a turtleneck shirt so the marks on my neck would be hidden. It was the first time I realized why I owned so many turtleneck shirts.

Not long afterwards, my mother caught Dave inside the bathroom with me. He tried rushing his assault on me and when he attempted to rush back out the bathroom door, the door hit his foot and he whacked his face into the door. Giving himself a bump on his head and being caught by my mother who came upstairs due to my screaming. I was crying by the time I walked out of the bathroom and into the hallway where my mother and Dave were. "No more tubs," my mother declared in a loud voice as if she was putting her foot down and declaring a victory. "You hear me?" she talked stern to Dave as she leaned into his face with a smirk on her face. I knew it was just an act my mother was playing.

My mother was now having me take baths only when she was

home. There were times when she would tell me, "I'm going to fold my laundry upstairs, so you can take your tub then." If Dave was home then my mother was now staying upstairs while I took my bath. As another school season came to an end, I flunked my year of school and had to attend summer school if I wanted to be promoted with my class to the 6th grade or I would have to repeat the 5th grade again. It was easier to stay out later with daylight hours lasting longer. Allowing me to be able to stay out longer with my brothers or over a friend's house. My mother would be home shortly after I had to be in for the night, causing Dave to lose out on his time with me and a lot of arguments between them both.

My mother insisted I was causing a lot of trouble in the home because of my behavior around Dave. Whether we were home, out in public or visiting a friend of theirs, I was scared of that man. One night my mother drove me to her friend Theresa's house, telling me I was sleeping over for the night. I was expecting to play with her kid's when I got there but they were gone for the weekend with their dad. Theresa was so sweet and sincere towards me. She wanted me to talk about my home life, but I wouldn't. She wasn't pushy but did tell me many times, "If you want to talk I'm here." The whole night it was just me and Theresa. She let me stay up late, we played card games and she let me sleep in her daughters bed for the night. When I awoke the next morning, Theresa started again in her attempt to get me to talk about my home life. It bothered her that I wasn't an active ten year old like a ten year old should be. It bothered her that I was so quiet, on alert and I say sorry way more than a kid should. After breakfast she told me a story about bad men and how they make their victims be quiet. "If someone hurts you in a way you don't like would you tell your mother?" she questioned me a few times until I answered her, "Yes." I answered all her questions except when it came to questions regarding Dave. Those questions I looked at the floor and said nothing.

The more she talked to me, the more sincere she got with me until she questioned me, "Does Dave make you keep secrets with him?" I looked right at her as she reassured me it was ok to answer and so I nodded my head yes. "Oh no honey," she responded as she got up and hugged me.

She had tears in her eyes as she hugged me, said, "Oh honey," and hugged me again before looking at me as she questioned with tears in her eyes, "Do you see his penis?" I looked at her and answered, "Yes." She became anxious as she told me to, "Sit, play, go watch television," as she continued, "Oh honey I'm calling your mother, "Oh honey want a snack?" "That bastard will never touch you again," she talked as she was all over the place, pacing in her kitchen, calling my mother and letting me know I was safe in her home. I heard Theresa on the phone yelling at my mother, "What is he doing to her," "You're her mother," Theresa continued to yell into the phone. Then the phone hung up and Theresa told me my mother would be there shortly to pick me up. She told me what Dave does to me, "He won't do anymore," as she continued to reassure me, "You're not in trouble," "He is the one in trouble," she reassured me. Theresa hugged me about a hundred times as we waited for my mother to come pick me up. As the day went on I got about another hundred more hugs from her as she began to become impatient as to why my mother was taking longer than expected to get to her house. Theresa called my mother on the phone again, "Where are you?"

When early afternoon became late afternoon, Theresa had called my mother about five more times as we waited hours upon hours for my mother to come to Theresa's house. Finally later in the afternoon we heard a woman being loud outside. It was my mother running up the front stairs of Theresa's apartment. When Theresa opened her door my mother stood at her doorway, hollering at me, "Move it, lets go." My mother was in a rush because she had to get to work. She told Theresa I was a liar and they argued back and forth as I made my way out the door, down the stairs and into my mother's car. My mother's loud voice followed me out the door but my mother didn't come outside to her car until a few minutes after I did. She drove away from where Theresa home when suddenly, 'SLAP,' my mother whacked her hand against my face and upside of my head. "What the heck did you say to her?" my mother questioned me as she was so disgusted, disappointed and so very mad. "I didn't tell her anything," I cried to my mother and I honestly didn't know what I did wrong, I didn't know why my mother was so mad at me when her friend was so nice to me. I didn't understand it and I was very confused. "Wait, you're going to work?" I questioned my mother who while yelling at me made the comment I was making her late for work. "Yes I have to work," she answered me as she continued to belittle me about what I said to her friend Theresa. (It would be another eleven years before I saw my mother's friend Theresa again.)

"Please don't leave me with him?" I pleaded to my mother as she drove down Pleasant Street to our home. My mother didn't answer me as she parked the car and walked in the front door. I followed behind her where Dave met us in the front hall. "She has a big mouth," my mother said to Dave as she just as quickly walked back out the front door and headed to work.

Standing in the front hallway I just as quickly started up the stairs to head to my bedroom when Dave quickly ordered me back down the stairs. "Now," he angrily hollered as his eyes widened. I didn't want to upset him so I went down the few steps I climbed and back to the front hallway where Dave was still standing. He positioned me in front of him, then he escorted me into the cellar. I didn't fight him going down the cellar stairs because I always made him trip, stumble or fall down them when I did try to fight causing me to get hurt even more. I walked down the stairs with Dave ordering me every step of the way. I was already crying in fear as he chained me to the cement area where the hot water tank was. He gave me a lecture about, "Girls who don't listen." He screamed in my face as he got angrier the more I screamed and cried. He smacked my head hard enough to stop me from screaming but not from crying. He handed me a white cloth and told me to wipe my tears telling me he'd be back down in a few minutes. "You better be done crying when I get back," he ordered, demanded and threatened me as he headed upstairs. Numerous times he ran upstairs to check on my sister or my brothers who we could hear coming in and out of the front door by the noises we heard from the cellar. I started to scream one time he headed up the cellar stairs but he came back down and stuffed a rolled up sock in my mouth. All I could do was cry. At one point he saw the tears pouring down my face and got very mad that I was still crying.

1975-1982 Lowell Massachusetts

He took the sock out of my mouth and forced me up to my knees. He tilted my head backwards so I was looking up to him. "Open your fucking mouth," he ordered me but it was the only thing that wasn't chained on me, so I refused to open my mouth. I moved my head, kept my mouth closed and did anything I could to keep him from attacking me again. Because he wrapped the chain around me with a padlock, I was unable to move, to run or to defend myself. Dave didn't wait for me to stop crying as he stood in front of me, taking his penis out of his unzipped pants and grabbing me by a handful of my hair. He banged my head against the aluminum hot water tank behind me. Then he stuck his hand in my mouth as he stretched my mouth open, shoving his penis inside. He banged my head, he banged himself into my face all while smacking me upside my head. "I'm feeling teeth," "That's it," "Stop with your fucking teeth," he ordered me as he would stop to stretch my mouth open again and again. Shoving his penis inside again and again. "I'm feeling teeth again," he angrily said as he got aggravated with me for giving him a hard time. With the chains on my feet and wrist, I would fling my head and try to close my mouth but his strength was too much for me. It seemed like it lasted for hours, days, years or an eternity. When he was finally done, he stepped away from me and I fell slumped onto the cold cellar floor, like a sack of potatoes that fell off a shelf. My head, mouth and neck hurt so much. My arms, legs and body hurt from fighting him so much, a fight I lost.

I must have fallen asleep because I could hear my mother was home from work and I started crying and screaming again until the cellar door opened. My mother and Dave came down the cellar stairs. And there was my mother looking at her ten year old daughter chained to a cement block in the cellar. Dave was all proud as he told my mother, "She's got to learn." They stood before me and gave me a lecture about telling lies.

They both came to the decision to leave me down there for the night so I could learn my lesson. As they went to head back up the cellar stairs, I started to scream. Dave came over and stuffed the dirty sock back in my mouth. But my mother kicked in her mother instincts when she insisted I would choke with the sock stuffed in my mouth. She then came over to me, took the sock out of my mouth, tied it around my head and across my mouth. I cried and cried and cried. My mother came down a little while later to bring me a blanket and tried reassuring me, "It's just for tonight." All I could do was give her dirty looks. I used the blanket as a pillow and laid on the sanded, cold, cement cellar floor. I cried, I hurt and I felt a pain that I had no idea what it was, I was only a kid. I prayed to my grandmother and I prayed to God to come get me, I just wanted to die. I felt a warming sensation as I cried until I fell asleep.

I woke up to my mother coming down the cellar stairs with some juice for me. "What do you want for breakfast?" she questioned me as she untied the sock from my head. "Mom unchain me," I yelled. "Mom let me go," I continued yelling at her. She just walked back up the cellar stairs. I started crying again, but then my mother came back down minutes later with a key in her hand. "Just go straight up to your room," she said to me as she unlocked the padlock and loosened the chain around me. "He's not happy I'm letting you go," my mother continued to say. I did exactly what she said to do. I ran up the cellar stairs, up the other set of stairs and straight into my bedroom. I listened as I heard my mother and Dave arguing over me. Then they both walked into my bedroom and gave me another lecture about saying things that are untrue and how I was grounded for causing trouble with my mother's friend Theresa. I stayed in my room the rest of the day wondering what I did that was so wrong? Why did my mother hate me? Why did Dave hate me? Why didn't my brothers care? Why can't I just be a good daughter? A good stepdaughter?

I had summer school the next day and had to walk there. It was being held at the Edith Rogers school where I had gone to school when we first moved to Pleasant Street. Summer school was held in one classroom of the school. The cracks and creaks of the wooden floors sounded real loud in a school with not many kids in it during the summer months. I don't think I heard one word the teacher said that day in class, but only because I was starting to question myself, 'Why wasn't my mother stopping Dave like she said she would?' 'Was my mother allowing Dave to hurt me?' I questioned myself many times. I was a very confused kid. I started keeping to myself, not wanting to hang out with anyone and just walking around my neighborhood whenever my mother worked so I wouldn't be home with Dave. Walking one Saturday morning I walked and walked until finally I was walking back down Pleasant Street on the opposite side of the street from where I lived. I met a girl named Sandi, who was hanging out front on her steps. I was ten years old and she was eleven years old. As summer went into full swing, Sandi and I would hang out a few times playing Barbie dolls, singing outside on her front porch and dreaming of being an ice skater just like Dorothy Hamill.

Summer school was real hot some days. We had bad thunderstorms one day and the whole classroom went dark. Then loud booms and crackle in the sky, an everlasting supply of good ole New England humidity was left in its wake. At home I was hanging out with Sandi a lot more but she had to be in early every night, so I started to hang out with other kids on the street. With school out for summer, there were a lot of kids on Pleasant Street in 1980. We would play games in the street of blackjack, dodgeball, kickball, bike riding, skateboarding or skipping rocks behind the Old Mother Hubbard pet food company where the Concord River flows. But as my mother worked nights and Saturdays, Dave continued to call me in early or grab me when I ran inside the house to get a toy or run to the bathroom. He would put choke holds on me more and more, each time slapping my face to wake me up.

I came home from summer school one day and my mother stopped me in the upstairs hallway. "You started your friend?" my mother whispered into my face with a smirk and laugh. "My what?" I answered my mother with a question as I continued to walk by her. "Your friend, you started your friend," she said as she moved in closer to me, still with that smirk and laugh. "What are you talking about?" I questioned her again, this time with a sarcastic tone. "Your menstrual period," my mother said. I questioned her, "What is that?" My mother gave me her mother/daughter talk as she explained it was, "A monthly thing where women pee blood every month." I gave her a strange look as I said, "I'm ten years old and I'm a kid." I gave my mother a disgusted look as I walked away from her and into my bedroom. She came into my room shortly afterwards, "Here go put this between your peewee and underwear," she said as she handed me a folded towel. "What?" I questioned her, "What's that?" I questioned her again without taking the big white folded thing from her hand and giving her a very confused look. "Your underwear had blood on them when I did laundry," my mother said to me. "Oh my God," I yelled at my mother, "It's your boyfriend," I screamed, but she just shook her head no at me. "Nope, no its not," my mother insisted. Informing me, "I was seven years old when I started," she said to me. Then my mother got nasty towards me, slapped me, held her hand against me and ordered me to stop telling lies about Dave. She threw what she called a maxi pad at me and sent me to the bathroom. I walked out feeling like I had a bed mattress between my legs. "Do they even make them for kids?" I questioned my mother but she just laughed, handed me a couple more and went downstairs. I wore the mattress between my legs for about an hour before going to the bathroom so I could remove it from my underwear. I took the other ones my mother gave me downstairs. "I don't have a menstrual thing, I have a your boyfriend won't leave me alone thing," I said to my mother as I folded my arms, standing there waiting for her to respond. "Cathy don't start," she snapped at me. "But mom," I quickly said back to her and then she said what she said best, "Go play." By the time summer school was over and it was time to go camping back at Wyman's beach, my attitude towards my mother and Dave was just brushed off as me being a, "Disrespectful brat," my mother called me constantly. Being slapped across the face or grounded at the campsite didn't change the fact that I wanted nothing to do with Dave.

I was constantly being grounded at the campsite for being fresh by screaming the word no in my mother's face each and every time she questioned me to do something with Dave. I would play with my sister a lot but my mother's failed attempts to get me to be nice to Dave caused her to take away my campsite privileges. First she took my hacky sack away, then she took playing cards away and then she took my baby sister away. "You don't deserve to play with her," my mother told me. It was impossible for

Dave to attack me at camp because our campsite was on Chipmunk Trail, a dead end road at the campground with campers on both sides. And I knew Dave couldn't assault me there so I would be a smartass kid causing a lot of dirty looks from Dave and a lot of slaps across my face or upside my head from my mother.

Even though I was grounded, when Dave was at work my mother would let me go swimming and bike riding. I just had to be back at camp by the time Dave got back from work. One day I was at the main beach with my brothers when I saw Sandi there with her family. We played together for the day. Next thing her and her mom were walking to my campsite to ask my mother if I could sleep over their house. I begged my mother, "Please mom, you have to work tonight," and my mother quickly said yes before I could say something about not wanting to be with Dave while she worked. I packed a bag of clothes and left Wyman's beach with my friend Sandi and her family as we headed back to Pleasant Street for my sleepover at her house. It was weird being on Pleasant Street and not being at my house. Sandi and I had a lot of fun. I spent two nights at Sandi's, we sang out on her porch to Shawn Cassidy, 'Da doo Ron Ron Ron,' and played with barbie dolls

My mother had planned to pick me up when she got out of work and before she headed back up to camp. When she picked me up, I got in her car and she declared in a loud voice, "This is going to stop right now." I looked at her weird and said, "I had fun at Sandi's," as I widened my eyes at her, waiting for her to say something, but nope, nothing. After a brief moment of silence my mother continued again, "Cathy this is going to stop right now," she said in a calmer voice. "No more secrets, no more lies," she continued, "No more lying, there's going to be respect from now on," she said as her voice got a little louder. That was when I caught on to what she was saying. "Wait, respect," I said to my mother and not waiting for her to speak, "Oh my God you're talking about me," I yelled at her. She snapped at me, "Of course I'm talking about you," "Who did you think I was talking about?" my mother questioned me with a giggle. My eyes filled with tears, my head shook as I looked out the window. I wanted to scream in her face, "Your boyfriend," but I didn't. My mother continued blabbing to me but I wasn't listening to her. "Are you letting him hurt me?" I questioned her and instead of answering me she slapped me as she drove, yelling at me for the stories I make up.

As soon as we got back to camp, my winner of a mother had to draw attention by declaring, "The brat is back," as we got out of the car. My mother was totally on Dave's side ever since the incident with her friend Theresa. Or maybe it was me finally realizing my mother was not stopping Dave from hurting me. I was becoming very fresh towards my mother and Dave at camp and being fresh also caused me to be grounded the whole month long camping trip.

I watched my mother joke around with Dave as she made a mockery out of me. Criticizing me for being the only one who has a problem with Dave. Snapping at me all while portraying me as a disrespectful brat. Humiliating me as she demanded I show proof of what Dave does to me. Belittling me as she told me I had no proof. Insulting me as she insisted people look down on kids who are abused. Leaving me worthless, lost and confused as a ten year old could be.

Once home from camping, school started, I passed summer school by a very small margin and was able to follow my class to 6th grade. I was back at the Oakland/Leblanc school and back to keeping my distance from Dave, not making eye contact with him, staying outside while my mother was at work and sleeping out when I could. Being a kid, it wasn't always an easy task to accomplish. I told my mother numerous times a day, "Mom I am scared of him." But it only made her more disgusted, frustrated and aggravated with me. I started hanging with another girl named Toni who lived just three houses down on the same side of the street. She came from a big family and we got along awesome. I'd sleep over her house all the time, I'd go babysitting with her to one of her older siblings' homes and sleeping over there also. I'd walk with her while she did her daily paper route. I'd take walks downtown with her so she could pay her newspaper bill at central savings bank in Zayre's parking lot on Church Street. She would buy me lunch at Espresso pizza or a string of bowling at the Rialto

1975-1982 Lowell Massachusetts

bowling lanes. We always checked out the rock shirts and 45's at Record Lane. We walked the streets from Pleasant to Central Street like we owned them and as kids, I'd like to think we did. We would stay up and do all nighters just sitting up listening to WAAF radio station or albums of Reo Speedwagon, Aerosmith, Journey and many more.

I had chores that wouldn't get done because I was either attacked by Dave as I tried or I stayed outside so I wouldn't be. It caused arguments between my mother and Dave because she wouldn't punish or ground me for not doing the chores. One Friday afternoon I was quickly getting my clothes packed to go sleep over Toni's house so we could go downtown on Saturday morning. My mother was also working that night, so no way I was staying home with Dave. I knew my baby sister was safe from Dave because my mother instilled in me she was his blood. As I was in my room getting my stuff together Dave came to my doorway and said, "Your mother wants to see you before she leaves." I just looked away from him and said, "Ok." I knew it meant she was ready to leave for work. I grabbed my stuff and headed out my bedroom towards the stairs. "She's in her bedroom," Dave said as I walked past him. I made a quick turn and walked into her bedroom but she wasn't in there. I quickly turned around to walk out when I walked into Dave who blocked me and squished me up against his bedroom door. Calling me, "A fucking brat," while pulling my pant pocket open and stuffing loose change in it. Then he did the same to my other pocket all while squishing me to the door and calling me names, "Stupid fucking retard," "Dumb fucking idiot." He threw a jar on his bed and I think the change he put in my pockets came from it. But his arm squishing me blocked my view as so did my tears. He pulled me into the upstairs hallway by my shirt and yelled downstairs for my mother to come upstairs.

When we saw my mother coming up the stairs, he said to her, "Look how she's been getting the money to go downtown every week," as he patted my pockets. Everything happened so fast as the loose change was yanked out of my pockets and my mother was whacking the shit out of me as I tried dodging her whacks. I walked out her bedroom, crying, hurting from the whacks I just endured as I made my way back to my bedroom. I didn't know what the heck happened as I just stared at my packed bag on my bedroom floor. What I did know, I was bawling my eyes out and I was grounded again. Before my mother left for work she came into my room and I told her, "Mom he put that money in my pockets," "He held me against your door and shoved it in my pockets." I continued to defend myself. But she didn't listen to a word I said. For a brief moment as my mother stood there speechless just looking at me, I thought she was finally going to do something about Dave, but that was only a brief moment as my mother gave a look that included rolling her eyes at me as she handed me a notebook and pencil. "What's this for?" I questioned her. With a look of disgust on her face she said, "Five hundred times, I want you to write an apology to Dave." "Oh my God, you're kidding right?" I yelled at my mother as I was in total confusion, disbelief and shock listening to what she was saying to me. "I want it done when I get home," my mother demanded as she left my bedroom and headed off to work.

My constant bitching to my mother about why I was grounded for all the wrong reasons, why I didn't want to be home with Dave, why I asked about going to my dad's, my uncle's, my older sister's or my mother's friend Theresa, were all answered by my mother's insulting and degrading reasons as to why I could not go to any of the above named. My mother told me my dad moved to Atlantic City to get away from me, my uncle was dead, my older sister didn't like me and her friend Theresa wants an apology letter also. Then she told me to write one hundred times to her friend Theresa, 'I will not lie to you again.' I had no choice but to do what I was told.

My school had a scavenger hunt field trip. It was a week-long camping adventure that included a lot of fun and cranberry bogs. Parents had to drive their kids to the school on the day of the field trip and of course it came with bitching from my mother about having to drive me to school. On the way there I again tried to plead with my mother about Dave. I told her I was afraid in my own house and I was afraid of Dave. "He forces me mom," I told her but she just got disgusted with me as she asked me questions, "What would he want with a little kid?" "Where do you come up with these stories?" Ending her disappointment in me with, "Come on huh," as she refused to talk anymore about it. I pleaded with my mother to call the police on him while I was gone, "I won't tell them you always knew," I said to her and that did not go over well with her or should I say me. "Knew What?" my mother snapped at me, then she bitched and complained the whole ride to my school. A couple of big yellow buses drove us to our destination which was a long drive. I made a lot of friends in my neighborhood, school, teachers liked me, friends parents liked me and now the camp counselors liked me. I was picked to be the helper in hiding items throughout the area. It wasn't so I could help hide things, it was so I could talk with a counselor about my home life. My teacher was the one who set it up, Mrs. Farrell.

I became silent when it came to talking about my home life. I truly believed I would be causing trouble if I told on Dave. So I concentrated on the fun at camp. We sang songs, went hiking, played games, went on trips to bogs and then it was time to go home. I questioned them if I could stay but they said I couldn't. On the way home my teacher sat next to me to tell me how when we headed to camp a week earlier all the kids were crying and missing their homes. "But you weren't," she said to me. "Now we're heading home and nobody's crying but you," she continued as she questioned me, "Why?" I was crying because I was going to miss all those nice people at that camp and I answered my teacher, "Because I don't want to go home." But it was 1980, the rule was, 'You went home to your mother,' and home is where I went.

As the buses pulled up to the school, there were many parents standing outside their cars and waiting outside of the school. As we all prepared to exit out of the bus with our bags of dirty laundry and pillows from our week away, I looked for my mother but she wasn't there yet. As more and more kids were leaving, my mother still wasn't there. "Want me to call your mom?" a teacher questioned me. "No that's ok," I answered her. She giggled as she explained she was going to call my mother. "I'll give her a few more minutes," she continued to say as she looked at her watch on her wrist. Soon there were no kids and no buses at the school. The teacher went into the school right before the last of the teachers left, I think she may have called my mother. Soon there was just the teacher and myself. She talked to me about the field trip and how much fun it was. Then we heard the screeching of tires as my mother came driving fast up the street and slamming on her car brakes as she came to a stop in front of the teacher and myself. "Come on let's go," my mother yelled out her driver's side window. I assumed I was going to tell my mother about my field trip on the ride home, but she didn't want to hear it. She complained about having to come pick me up, about how her day was interrupted and how the troublemaker was back home. And home I was, where being grounded resumed.

Dave was using every opportunity of me being grounded to have his ways with me. One day he informed me he was not happy when he came home from work and found out my mother let me go on a school field trip. He stood at the doorway of my bedroom, I was sitting on my bed, it was afternoon time and I thought my mother was home but she left for work without telling me. He was telling me how upset he was that I left without saying bye. Asking if I thought it was funny, asking if I was being sneaky and he went on and on as he stood there looking at me from my doorway. I wanted him to know I was listening to him because I didn't want him to hurt me. He kept asking and speaking quickly so I couldn't respond to him. "You think it was funny?" "You were being sneaky huh?" "Not even a goodbye," "Do you care about your family?" "I know you told someone," he continued. Then he shook his head, shrugged his shoulders, charged at me and said, "Let's go you fucking brat," as he clenched his hand around the back of my neck, lifting me off my bed as I squished to the pain of his hand lifting me. I wrapped my legs to his side as he walked through my doorway into the hallway and straight into his bedroom. I was trying to release the pain I was feeling as he carried me by the back of my neck until he flung me onto his bed. Where I endured another terrorizing, horrifying, vicious assault.

My school would call my mother about me falling asleep in class, not doing my homework, zoning out, being startled quickly and my bizarre story of my principal being a friend of Dave's. They would either solve it over the phone or have my mother come in for a meeting. My mother had me already described as a liar, a thief and a troublemaker to my school and it being the 1980s when, 'You went home with your mother,' I was always being sent home with her.

Dave began to lose his patience with me as I hid more, screamed louder, kicked harder and begged him to leave me alone each and every time. He was now ordering me away in front of my brothers, having them watch our baby sister while he ordered or carried me to his bedroom. Where he terrorized, tortured and raped me every night my mother worked, every Saturday morning she worked and worse when she worked a double shift or was at bingo. It would give him an extra hour with me on the nights she went to Bingo. He continued to do to me what he had been doing to me and forcing me to do for the past five years of my childhood already. No matter how much I fought him, gagged, cried and gave him a hard time. Sometimes it ended with that one slap, whack or bang that left me lying motionless, unable to move yet feeling everything that monster was doing to me. Hearing everything he was saying and trying not to hear him at the same time. Trying not to feel him as all I could do was cry and gaze into the tears of pain that flooded down my face. He was also now changing his way with me as he now wanted to, "Make a game out of it," he said one day. Ordering and taunting me to run around his bedroom. I'd run to any wall furthest from him, I'd run over his bed and I'd run under it trying to hide the furthest from his reach but he got me each and every time. I didn't know why my mother never stopped him? Why she let him move back in? Why she didn't believe me? Why she didn't protect me from him? I didn't know what my brothers heard on the other side of that bedroom door? With all the times Dave got loud with me or all my screams and cries, I didn't know what they thought about the closed door I was behind with a grown man? With every knock they knocked throughout all those years and I was inside, why didn't they care? I didn't know why Dave hated me as he did. No matter where I was playing outside, out front with other kids

ND
in the neighborhood, in the backyard with my brothers and baby sister, inside the house, the attic, bathroom, if I was sick, if I was sleeping, if I was hiding, Dave would always come get me. Making me pass out by choking me and then slapping my face to wake me as he laughed in my face with his evilness. He would spit on me, spit in my face and whack me upside my head reminding me how worthless I was. Reminding me no one cares about me. Reminding me I don't have long to live.

One day he told me he was going to be nice to me. "I'm going to be nice today," he said in an eagerly happy manner as I sat at the foot of his bed crying. He turned his back towards me and opened a drawer in his dresser bureau. "Today I will let you choose," he said as he turned around with his white leather belt in one hand and his penis out of his pants with his other hand. He told me again he was being nice and wanted me to stop crying, all while smacking me upside my head in an attempt to get me to stop crying as he angrily told me to choose, "Do you want this?" as he brushed his penis against me, "Or do you want this?" he continued as he flashed his white leather belt in my face.

"I don't have to remind you how much this hurts," he said to me as he laughed while shoving his belt in my face. He continued saying, "This," as he brushed his penis against me. "Or this," he happily continued as he became more angrier the longer it took me to answer. I cried harder and got smacked more as he angrily rushed me to answer his question of which one, I wanted. I finally answered but he wanted me to stop crying and answer him. I couldn't stop crying as I was bawling my eyes out so I pointed to his white leather belt. "The belt," I said in between my breaths of tears and mucus running down my face. He then questioned me again, "This or this?" he questioned over and over again all while brushing his penis against me and flashing his white leather belt in my face. I was now answering him every time, "The belt." He was not happy I picked the belt and proceeded to assault me. He flipped me backwards onto his bed, took my pants off and began rubbing his penis against my naked body while forcing himself inside me. Feeling him touch me as he proudly praised his progress for being able to go further inside me. He praised his progress because he was now able to push his brown plastic cigar holder and virgin Mary rubber thing inside me more. He praised himself for making me bigger, a little at a time. "Not as much blood this time," he giggled.

When he was finished, he kicked me to get up, to get dressed and to get out of his room. I was hurting but I got up, I got dressed and once again Dave stopped me at the door. "You chose this," he said as he waved his white leather belt in the air. He threw me back onto his bed, tore my pants back off and proceeded to whack me with his leather belt on my bare buttocks. I didn't feel the pain from those whacks though, maybe because I was already hurting or I just became so accustomed to the pain. He continued to stretch my jaw or my legs apart until I agreed by nodding my head to keeping his secret. He would punch my stomach until I agreed. He would poke my head, twist my arms or squeeze my neck as he dangled me in the air, threatening to kill my brothers, my baby sister and me. Forcing me hundreds and hundreds of times to make the promise. And hundreds and hundreds of times, I promised him, although each and every time I told my mother.

My mother finally got sick of my complaining about Dave as she yelled one day, "I'm going to finally put an end to this." I instantly felt a happiness go through me as I was excited my mother was finally going to put an end to it. I followed her upstairs in excitement, into her bedroom where she went fishing through some bags in her closet. She came out with a package in her hand and I followed her out of her bedroom and into my bedroom. My mother's solution was not to call the cops nor was it to throw Dave out of the house. Her solution was a tiny lock hook she twisted into my door with the small circle hook twisted into the door frame. "There now you can lock it and keep everyone out," my mother snapped at me before walking out of my room and leaving me once again baffled at her motherless ways. Within a day that lock disappeared. My mother put another lock on my door and that one disappeared also. After the third latch hook lock disappeared, my mother was fed up and didn't put anymore locks on my door. My constant complaining of being left home with Dave while my mother worked caused her to allow me off punishment. "Only while I'm at work," my mother declared as if it was a victory for me.

One Saturday in early fall my mother called us all in for supper. It was a warm sunny day and my brothers wanted to get back outside. They rushed eating so I rushed to eat my dinner also. While we were doing that my mother left for work. I finished eating the same time as my brothers and Dave had us all put our plates in the sink before going out. After we placed our plates in the sink, the three of us headed to the front door. "Hey Cathy what's this?" Dave questioned me as my brothers went out the door. I turned to see what he was referring to when my head went down and I was instantly in a headlock as I heard the front door slam shut. "No, no, no," I pleaded as I started crying while my feet dragged across the floor. He flung me by the headlock hold he had on me as he held me against the kitchen sink. He held me with his leg and one arm while he unlocked the cellar door. I tried so hard not to be back down in that cellar. I flung everything I could, my hands, arms, legs, feet, head, neck and my body as I attempted to try and break free of his strength. But like the years and assaults prior, I was unable to. I was slammed against the cellar door as I reached for a grip but he just picked me up, carried me in front of himself and down the cellar stairs. My long skinny legs got in the way and we tumbled down at least six of those stairs. He also got hurt and he was mad. He flung me onto a bench he had in the cellar and tied me with rope to the end of the bench. "You fucking move I'm going to kill ya," he said as he headed back up the cellar stairs yelling, "Fuck." I was scared shit of that guy and I did what he said, I didn't fucking move. He came back downstairs a few minutes later and stood in front of me. All I stared at was his work boot and didn't dare look up at him. "Stop fucking crying," he said angrily as he bent down so he was able to say it into my face. "I was going to let you live until your twelfth birthday," he laughed. "I don't know now," "Your nothing but trouble," he insisted. "Big fucking mouth," he continued saying to me while drinking from his beer can, smoking his cigarettes and smacking me upside my head. When all of a sudden, we heard my mother upstairs coming in the

1975-1982 Lowell Massachusetts

front door and hollering, "Hey who's with the baby?" Dave quickly pointed his finger in my face, "Shut your mouth," he said to me before he ran up the cellar stairs. I heard the cellar door shut and I screamed. The cellar door opened and my mother came down the cellar stairs. "What, what's going on here?" she questioned as she untied the rope and told me, "Go play," as she rushed me away from the bench and towards the stairs. She yelled at Dave, "What the heck are you doing?" I heard her say as I booked it up the cellar stairs. I ran into the front hall, out the front door and straight across the street where I sat on the sidewalk curb waiting for my mother to come outside. It wasn't long before she came outside and headed to her car. "Are you still going to work?" I questioned as I ran over to my mother. "Yes," she said along with, "No more going down cellar with him," she declared before closing her car door and driving away.

I'd try to make sure I wasn't home or around when my mother worked. When suddenly my mother gave me more chores to do around the house and chores that had to be done or I would be grounded. "You're old enough now," she said to me, "No more stupid excuses," she continued. Adding to my chores of keeping my room clean and doing the dishes, my mother added folding clothes and vacuuming. They very rarely got done because I was too busy hiding or running out the door so I was safe from Dave.

I hid outside under the back porch; it was gross but I buried my face into my folded arms and stayed there until I heard it was safe to sneak out. Then I walked around the neighborhood or waited on the curb across the street until my mother got home. I hid inside the dryer, folded like a snowball until I heard my mother was home from work and popped out of the dryer where my mother questioned, "What are you doing in there?" I answered her, "Because of Dave." I hid behind his recliner chair for hours one Saturday. He got up looking for me, hollering my name, getting himself a beer and sitting back down. He questioned my brothers to go find me. But I stayed there until my mother got home and then I popped out from behind it while he was still sitting in it. I hid in his bedroom closet one day for almost four hours until I heard my mother's voice in her room and walked out to my mother asking me, "What are you doing in my closet?" I pointed to Dave who was looking at me surprised and said, "Why don't you ask him," "I've been hiding in there since you left for work," I told her and my mother yelled, "Go play," as she whipped her hands at me to scoot me out of her bedroom. I hid under both my brother's beds and my bed squishing furthest away from his reach for many hours as I either waited for my mother to get home or got busted by a brother for being in their room. I hid behind the washer machine, squishing myself between it and the wall until my mother got home.

On two separate occasions one of my eyes connected to one of Dave's elbows during an assault and my mother made me pass it off as a pigsty. I didn't even know what it was. She made me wear Vaseline over my eye and one time made me put the actual medicine for a sty on my eye. My bruises from Dave were easily hidden through clothes, as they were mostly between my thighs, my back and upper arms. Not having my chores done and not being home or being around because I was hiding so well caused my mother and Dave to argue about why I wasn't being grounded for being disrespectful to him. My mother was being pulled on both ends. He was telling her to ground me and she would come into my room to talk me into being grounded, "To make him happy," she'd say to me in an attempt to agree with Dave and be grounded. I'd yell at her, "I'm not staying home with him while you work." She would just walk out the door like she's done so many times before. Whenever my mother left the house to go to work, I was trying to either already be outside or following her out the door. She always yelled but I was already used to it. I was learning to block her out, I guess. Soon it was December 1980, I turned eleven years old and my birthday was no different than any other. My mother was now buying smaller size maxi pads and then shame me into silence, "Don't go blabbing about having your monthly friend," my mother told me, "Your friends will know what happened to you," she continued as she slowly instilled in me that it was my fault Dave was hurting me. I just looked at her in disbelief, "How could you mom?" I questioned her. "Happens, it's happening not just happened," I yelled at her, but again she walked away.

1975-1982 Lowell Massachusetts

CHRISTMAS time was here again and what would be my last Christmas with my family as I continued to fight to not be tortured, raped and abused by Dave anymore.

An uninterested child on Christmas morning would tell any adult that something was wrong with that child. As my mother continued to tell me to open my gifts on Christmas morning, I was more petrified of the man sitting in the same room as us than I was about wanting to open the gifts around the tree. I stayed upstairs in my room most of the day to avoid being around Dave who was downstairs. During Christmas school vacation my mother drove us all to a building on Market Street in regards to food stamps or housing. There were a lot of people there, a lot of kids with parents in a wide square office with huge windows showing the street outside. My mother had us sit on some chairs by the window and we were there for a while. My brothers and I were getting restless with the long wait. I turned around in my seat and looked out the large size windows. I watched as cars drove by, as people walked by and as birds flew by. There were snow piles on the sidewalks but it was from the snow days earlier. It was a sunny winter day and then there he was, I looked, I zoomed in on that look and, "Yup that's my dad," I said as I jumped from my seat, ran to my mother and tugged at her shirt. "Mom it's my dad, can I go get him?" I questioned her as I ran towards the door of the building before my mother answered me. I ran after him; I was so excited that I climbed over the small snow banks instead of around them. After I made sure it was ok to cross Adams Street, I booked it across and there was my dad just a few feet away. "Well come on," he hollered with a smile on his face. He waited for me to catch up to him. He hugged me, picked me up and questioned me, "Where have you been?" "Every time I call your mother, she says you're out," he continued. I looked at him confused as I told him, "My mother said you moved to Atlantic City." He then looked at me with a confused look on his face. We got to his front door, he put me down and we walked into his home. "Look what I found on my travels," my dad said to my stepmother. She came right over and gave me a hug. Then my dad questioned me about why I said he moved to Atlantic City. I told him what my mother told me and I told him about her driving to the wrong set of brick apartments a year earlier. I told him how I always ask about him, "But my mother always has excuses," I told him. Then we heard my mother's car horn going off outside. My dad quickly questioned if I wanted to sleep over and I said, "Yes."

He went outside where he and my mother got into an argument. He yelled, she yelled and my stepmother shut the door so we didn't have to hear them. When my dad came back in, he handed me a pile of Christmas gifts. "We buy them every year," my dad said to me. "We just donate them when I don't hear from you," my dad continued as I opened my gifts. Pajamas, crafts and a real pretty pink sweater with thin strips of purple, blue and green colors across it. I kept myself busy up in the room I slept in at my dad's. Playing with my new craft sets, puzzles and coloring books my dad and stepmom got me for Christmas. Even knowing they may have to donate them, they continued to buy me gifts. I thought that was really cool. So many times, I wanted to tell my dad about Dave but I was afraid of the consequences if I told. I was afraid to bring it up to my dad because I didn't want him to look down on me if I told him. I was afraid to tell my dad because I didn't know how to explain it all. My dad made plans for us to do things the next day but my mother was there first thing in the morning.

We made plans for me to sleepover the following weekend. "The whole weekend," my dad said and I agreed. He walked me to my mother's car and told my mother I was sleeping over the following weekend. "If she can behave herself," my mother said loudly as to make the notion I was a troublemaker. I knew I was in trouble when I got home for taking off on my mother the day before when I chased my dad and left my mother with no choice but to let me sleep over. My mother drove away not saying a word to me. The ride was very quiet when suddenly, 'Whack,' right upside my head. "That's for running off," my mother yelled at me. Instead of crying from the whack upside my head, I smiled. 'I ran off and won,' I thought to myself. 'It was my dad, I got to sleep over, I have toys there now and I was sleeping over again in six days,' I kept thinking to myself while smiling. Then I hear, "Cathy," my mother yelled at me as I looked at her. "Did you hear a word I said?" she questioned me as she continued driving home. I answered her, "Yes," even though I didn't hear a word she said. For the next six days my mother would criticize, ridicule, belittle and mock me as she would say things in front of Dave, "Cathy thinks her father is a better father," "Cathy looks so pitiful," "Cathy thinks she's better than everyone else," "Cathy thinks she's special," "Cathy wants attention," my mother continued with her cruel and nasty ways. I felt like such an outcast in that home.

I was excited to go to my dad's and spend the weekend there. I asked my mother if I could buy my dad and stepmother a Christmas gift. She wasn't happy but she took me to Sears department store on Plain Street and let me buy my dad a flannel shirt but wouldn't let me buy for my stepmother. My mother wasn't happy I found my dad again but there was nothing she could do about it. Finally something my mother couldn't take away from me, my dad, or at least I thought. Friday was finally here, I came home from school, packed my bag and booked it downstairs to where my mother was. "Can you drive me to my dad's?" I questioned her. "Jesus Christ Cathy," she bitched as she complained, "You just got home from school." Telling me she was waiting for Dave to get home from work so she didn't have to bring my baby sister for the ride. I was mad, I wanted to leave before he got home. Instead, I went up to my room until I heard him come home from work. I then went downstairs to where my mother was, "Can we go now?" I questioned her. "Jesus Christ Cathy," she yelled, "Everybody must starve because of you?" she questioned me as she continued to yell, "I have to cook supper first," she told me, causing me to stomp my feet while walking up the stairs to my bedroom. I was so mad and sat in my bed being pissed off until finally my mother hollered up for me. I headed out my bedroom to run down the stairs, but I was blocked by Dave who shoved me back into my room. "You tell your father anything, I'll kill them all," he warned me. "You got it?" he questioned, "I'll kill everyone here then I'll go to your dad's place," "You want me to do that?" he continued to frighten me. I answered him, "I know, I'm not saying anything." Then he let me walk out of my bedroom and downstairs to eat supper. I walked into the kitchen to get some food but my mother stopped me, "Let's go," she hollered at me. She was ready to drive me to my dad's home. "You can eat at your fathers," she said to me. I ran back upstairs to retrieve my bag of clothes for my sleepover. I shut the door, down the few front steps and into my mother's car where she was warming it up from the cold January weather of 1981.

I was super excited to go to my dad's house and on the ride there my mother managed to degrade, belittle and ridicule me as she explained, "It already happened and nothing you can do about it," she said in regards to the abuse I endured. "I said something to him," "He won't have fun with you anymore," my mother continued with her excuses and defending Dave as she has for the past six years of my childhood. "Don't go blabbing to your father about what goes on at home," my mother continued with a smile to her face. "He'll want nothing to do with you if he knew you were molested," my mother insisted with her motherly words of non-wisdom and smirks. I was horrified, I didn't want my dad to hate me, I didn't want Dave to kill everyone, I knew I wouldn't be telling my dad anything about my home life.

I was finally at my dad's house and slept over for two nights. He told me so much while I was there. My dad was a proud Irish man. He told me about two sister's and two brother's I had on his side of my family. He told me my grandmother was actually his mother. He took me to the Sac club. We also walked over to where my godfather lived for a quick unexpected visit. My dad also explained that he had three kids from his first marriage and a daughter in Oklahoma. My dad never said anything bad about my mother in front of me but I did hear him say to my stepmother, "I don't know why she keeps her from us." He was referring to my mother keeping me away from them. I had more gifts on my bed at my dad's, a new blanket, slippers and more puzzles. I really wanted to tell my dad everything, but again I was scared. I didn't want to ruin the good time by bringing up something I didn't know how to explain. How does an eleven-year-old explain all she's been through? Where do I start? How do I carry the guilt if Dave did kill who he said he would? How do I carry the shame my mother instilled in me of being degraded because I was molested?

1975-1982 Lowell Massachusetts

I played board games with my dad all day, checkers, life and card games. Later that night I met my dad's oldest daughter who was with her son and he was spending the night with us. He was my nephew and as always, it was a lot of fun at my dad's that weekend. I overheard him being concerned about me to my stepmom. "She says sorry too much," "She's too jumpy," "I have to win her trust again," he continued to say, when they noticed I heard them I got double the hugs and some cereal for breakfast. Sunday morning came and my mother called to say she was on her way to pick me up. My dad explained to me he was going into the hospital in three days and I wouldn't be able to stay over next weekend but I would be staying over in two weeks. My dad made sure I was listening to him as he said with a smile, "Catherine," as he motioned his finger to his eye and to me. Going back and forth doing it a few times until we both laughed. "I will be waiting for you," he said assuring me that I will be coming back. He gave me big hugs along with my stepmother who was always giving me double the hugs.

When my mother picked me up, she beeped the horn and continued to beep the horn until I came outside. She didn't even care about my weekend at my father's. I tried telling her, but there was just silence from her as she drove. Then I blurted out, "When I stay at my dad's in two weeks, I am asking him if I can live with him and my stepmother."

That caused my mother to snap at me, "You should have just stayed," I explained to her about him having to go into the hospital for a few days, but my mother just snapped at me again, "Too bad." She drove home to where I wouldn't see my father again until June of 1983. Once we were back home my mother quickly let it be known to Dave how I wanted to go live with my dad. "She thinks her father is better than you," my mother said to him. I tried to defend myself as I yelled, "I never said that." But my mother went on, "He's no different than your father is," my mother said as she compared my father to her monster boyfriend. She continued being nasty to me, speaking with a nasty expression on her face, "You look so pitiful," she snapped at me. "You just want attention," "Cathy thinks the grass is greener on the other side," she continued speaking in her attempt to ridicule me. I remember thinking to myself how the grass was greener on my neighbor's side of the fence and not understanding why my mother said that to me.

My mother was making me an outcast in my own home as she continued to ridicule, belittle, mock and shame me for not wanting to be abused by Dave anymore. There was only one week left until I was going to sleep at my dad's again and I pretty much stayed in my room after school and on the weekend. So many times, a day I tried to understand why my mother wasn't stopping Dave or protecting me. I knew I wasn't coming back after I went to my father's again so I sucked it up for one more week. Until a few days later when I was sitting in my room reading a book and my bedroom door came flying open. My mother charged inside my room and not towards me, she charged straight for my dresser bureau which was on the opposite side of my bedroom. As she kneeled down to open one of my drawers, I questioned her, "What are you doing?" She pulled something out of my bottom drawer and turned to me yelling, "Your freaking grounded," she yelled as she whacked me with her hands, arms and a glass jar filled with loose change. She just kept whacking me until finally storming out of my bedroom and leaving me there on my bed, crying and wondering, 'What the heck?'

After calming down on my crying, I walked into my mother's room where she was in bed with Dave watching television. I walked to my mother's side of the bed and I told her, "Mom I didn't put that in my drawer." But my mother quickly snapped, "Then who did, the boogeyman?" she questioned. I continued to tell her, "Mom I didn't do it," "He must have," I said as I pointed to Dave. He shot me a dirty look and my mother yelled at me to go to my room because I was once again grounded. I went to my room where I didn't let it bother me because I was going to my dad's that coming Friday and I wasn't coming back. I knew Dave and my mother were never going to hurt me anymore. As the week went by Friday was finally here. I got home from school, packed my bag and waited a little bit to ask my mother to drive me to my dad's because after all, I just got home from school. Soon it was supper time and my mother said nothing about driving me to my dad's. So I worked up the nerve to ask her to drive me, "Mom can you drive me to my dad's now?" My mother looked at me, rolled her eyes at me and said, "Your grounded." I quickly responded, "For something I didn't do again." Then I said, "My dad is expecting me to be there today, mom," I pleaded to her.

I knew there was nothing she could do to stop me from going to my dad's because he was expecting me there, because he wanted me there, because he loved me being there. "No sir," my mother said as she squished her face closer to me. "I called him and told him you were a thief and you were grounded," she said as she stood there smiling, waiting for me to respond or seeing my heart break right in front of her face. "What?" I yelled. "No mom, please mom," I begged her but she just yelled, hollered, waved her hands in the air and walked away after sending me to my room for, "Being fresh," she said. It was another night with no supper and no going to my dad's. I was so heartbroken, I cried and cried. I started to demand my mother give me my dad's phone number but she wouldn't. First, I would question her once a day, "Can I have my dad's phone number?" Then it went to twice a day, "Will you call my dad for me?" Then it was three times a day, "I want to call my dad," and I continued. Every day I would question my mother about me wanting to call my dad. My mother would tell me, "I called him and no one answered." Then she would say, "He's still in the hospital." Then she would tell me, "He's too busy," and she continued with her lies, "He's on vacation," "He doesn't want to see his thief of a daughter."

A check-up at Dr Kaplan's office led to another excuse my mother couldn't take me to my dad's. Dr Kaplan had ordered physical therapy in Boston Mass for my back, hips and legs. He yelled at my mother, "What's going on with this girl at home?" He yelled at her like he knew her. He apologized to me for scaring me as he could tell I was scared. He was very disappointed in my mother and soon my mother was dismissing me from school two days a week as we drove to Boston for my physical therapy. I was giving exercises, leg braces and a back brace I had to wear nightly. After receiving my leg braces, my mother got into an argument with a doctor there and suddenly all the trips to physical therapy stopped along with the back and leg braces disappearing. When I questioned my mother about it all, her excuse was, "Doctors are just being nosey doctors," and, "You don't need them braces anyways." That was the end of that, for my mother anyways. For me, it was only beginning because I was finally going to make Dave stop hurting me. I would also never see another doctor under my mother's care again.

When Dave first started assaulting me on Fletcher Street in 1975 at the age of five years old, he would get mad when I cried and fought him all the time. Now in 1981 at the age of eleven, he wanted me to cry and fight him as he started with a new game he called, "A fun game." He would say a number, tell me to go hide and start counting to the number he told me. I would huddle against a wall, crawl under beds only to be dragged back out, he would tear my clothes off as he hysterically laughed while doing to me what he's been doing to me for so many years, months, weeks, days and hours already. Sometimes choking me into blackouts then slapping my face until I awoke only to choke me again as he told me of all the trouble, I caused by not keeping my mouth shut. One Saturday morning I was still grounded, my mother was at work, my brothers were out and my baby sister was in her playpen. I was in my room when my closed bedroom door opened and I looked up to see Dave standing at my doorway. "You know the drill," he said to me as he motioned me out of my bedroom. "Come on, please no," I pleaded with him. "Don't make me walk over there," he said to me, causing me to step off my bed. "Let's go, you know the drill," he said again while motioning me out of my bedroom. "Please no," I pleaded as I walked out of my bedroom and tried running to the stairs.

He blocked me as he pushed me away from the stairs until I was inside his bedroom. "Calm down," he said to me. "This time I'll count higher," he said giggling. "It'll be fun," he continued. "You want to have fun, don't you?" he questioned me but I was afraid to answer because I didn't know what the right answer was without upsetting him. I first told him that I didn't want to have fun. He let me know, "I don't like your answer," and question me again, "Do you want to have fun?" I had no choice but to answer him yes. "See was that hard?" he questioned me. "Now I'll count to ten," he said to me as he explained I could hide anywhere in his bedroom, while he watched where I hid. My choices were under a bed, on the side of a bureau or in a closet he'll watch me go in. I pleaded with him, "No, not again." But he always overpowered me. When he was done assaulting me, he would now make me stand still in positions. Stand on one leg for hours, kneel while my knees were bent on a broomstick or he made me bark as I stood still, sometimes lasting for hours.

One night after viciously assaulting me, he made me stand in one spot for what seemed like an eternity while my body ached in pain. He noticed I kept looking at the clock on his nightstand table. "Well, your mother will be home soon," he said to me. "Go on," he said all happily while looking at me. "Go on, put on your clothes," he said while he motioned me to my clothes that rested all over the floor of his bedroom. I was crying and just wanted out of that room. I picked up my clothes, put them on as I cried and waited for his next demand. "Go on, you can leave," he said. I took off towards that bedroom door. But just as quickly as I made it to the bedroom door, Dave jumped off the bed and was in front of the door. He blocked me as he said, "I forgot to tell you something." He put his finger to his temple. "Oh ya," he giggled as he put his hands on my shoulders, kneeled down to my height and screamed, "She's working a double." I begged, pleaded, fought, screamed and bit as hard as I could. But his strength was just too powerful for me. Endless knocks on the bedroom door from my brothers did not protect me, my own mother did not protect me and soon no one older than me in that house would be able to deny the fact that Dave was in fact abusing me. As Dave turned his attacks into a game of cat and mouse chasing and terrifying an already terrified kid. A sickening horrifying reality knowing I am that kid.

I spent most of my 6th grade school year 1980-1981 being grounded. My school class photo has me in the front row and it shows the extremely sad eleven-year-old kid I was. In 1981 I started to question the way my mother allowed me to live. I was refusing to stay home with Dave when she worked. I would beg her to take me somewhere or off punishment and if she didn't, I was now chasing her out the door and refusing to go back inside the home until she got home. I would hang out with friends in the neighborhood and if no one was around, then I would walk all over the Belvidere section of Lowell. When the street lights came on, then I would walk back to Pleasant Street where I sat on the curb across the street from my home and ignore Dave as he called me in for the night. If he attempted to cross the street, I was already running by the time he stepped off the porch steps.

If I wasn't sleeping at a friend's house then I was setting my alarm clock on Friday nights so I was awake on Saturday mornings to run out the door with my mother as she left for work. Many times, my mother and Dave argued over me. He wanted me grounded and she kept letting me outside while she worked. On rainy days I would sneak out the back door and stay in the backyard. Hiding so Dave couldn't attack me. I purposely began tying my shoelaces in double knots just so he couldn't take them off when he would attack me. I was now wearing jeans under sweat pants and multiple articles of clothing which gave me more time to defend myself. I was eleven years old and these are the things I did to protect myself. I told my mother I couldn't do my homework because of Dave. I told my mother I didn't feel safe in my own home because of Dave. I told my mother I couldn't sleep at night because of Dave. I told my mother I couldn't go to the bathroom, do my chores, have friends over, not be scared, not be terrified in my own home because of Dave. When I was afraid of Dave hurting my baby sister, my mother always reminded me with her disgusted look on her face and say, "Come on huh she is his blood." Sometimes my mother would act a bit concerned, sometimes she would leave my bedroom determined to put a stop to Dave attacking me and sometimes she was fed up, disgusted and agitated with me still talking about things Dave was doing to me and making me do. If my brothers were home and he or they found me hiding, he would flip me over his shoulders and carry me to his bedroom. If I grabbed onto a doorway frame or stair banister, he would ask whoever was nearby to release my hand as he controlled my legs from kicking. I would scream, "He's raping me," as he carried me up the stairs. But they didn't take me seriously. Even while I was locked in a room with a grown man, they didn't take me seriously.

One afternoon when my mother was already at work, my brothers were out with their friends and I was walking around Pleasant Street when I had to use the bathroom. There was no holding it until my mother got home. I had no choice but to run inside my house, run up the stairs and into the bathroom. I was thinking, 'What a relief it was to pee.' When I was done, I flushed the toilet and headed back down the stairs. I was only down about two steps when I was pulled from behind. Everything flung sideways and then a, 'Puff,' sound as my face slammed onto my mother's bed. My head bounced from the impact as I felt my pants being pulled down as Dave made grunting noises. My legs started to sway as he tried taking my sneakers off but my pants got tangled at my ankles. Dave had a lot of trouble trying to take my pants and sneakers completely off. He became frustrated as he picked my head up from behind and whacked me upside my head. I instantly went limp, I just laid there on my stomach, folded over my mother's bed as Dave did what he wanted to do. He rubbed his sperm all over my back, my buttocks and my legs before kicking me as he ordered me, "Get the fuck out of my room." When my mother came home from work that day I was in my room and in my bed. She questioned me why I was already in bed and I once again told her what Dave did to me while she was at work. "I'll talk to him," she said before quickly walking out of my room.

My mother always cooked Sunday dinners and because her or Dave didn't work on Sunday's, I spent my Sunday's being grounded. There was a law about campers being parked on a street during winter months. I don't know what Dave did with his camper during the winter, but it was back in its spot on the corner of Porter and Pleasant Street by early spring 1981. One Sunday I was in my room reading when I stepped out to head to the bathroom. Next thing, I don't know if I felt or heard the loud heavy thump, but my eyes opened and everything was dark. I thought I was tied up but my arms moved. I was laying down but everything was so dark. I looked down to my feet and saw total darkness. I looked above my head and saw light. 'Wait I'm inside the camper,' I thought to myself as I raised my arms above my head and slid myself upward. Just as my head popped out of the tunnel I was in, Dave grabbed me by my cheeks, squeezing so hard my teeth cut my mouth inside. "I forgot my keys, don't you fucking move," Dave ordered me as he shoved my head back into the tunnel again. I heard the camper door shut and I quickly scooped myself back out of what I was in. As I looked at it, I realized it was a type of rolled up flooring. A 1970 style tile flooring with colors of yellow, brown and orange. Then I heard kid's outside on Porter Street. I sat on the bench inside the camper and thought to myself, 'Wait, he comes back he's taking somewhere I don't want to go.' Without hesitation I jumped up and booked it out of the camper. I ran across the street and passed Dave who was returning back to the camper. He gave me a dirty look but with too many kids outside playing, he was unable to grab me.

"Where the heck have you been?" my mother snapped at me when I walked into the house. She was in my face really mad at me. " I don't know, in the camper," I answered. Her composure changed as she looked at me strangely, "What do you mean the camper?" she questioned. I answered her, "I woke up wrapped in a floor." My neck was hurting and even though I didn't see what my neck looked like, it was burning. I flashed my neck to her, "he's still making me pass out," I told her. "He chokes me mom," I continued as I told her again how I was afraid in my own home. I was afraid to sleep, I was afraid to walk in my own home and I was afraid Dave was going to kill me. But nope, my mother insisted I was wrong. "He's a good man," she yelled at me in disgust as she insisted, I was damaging his reputation. It was now late in the afternoon and I was missing for over four hours my mother told me. She insisted I snuck out of the house and so I was grounded longer. My mother started lying about days she had to work. I would be in my room after school knowing my mother wasn't working because she told me she wasn't. Then I'd go downstairs to find she'd be gone, her car gone and Dave standing right in front of me. He would instantly start playing his game. If I begged him to stop it only gave me less time to run and hide. "I'll count to twenty," he would yell.

1975-1982 Lowell Massachusetts

"And you have two floors today," he'd continue to say in excitement as he instantly started to count. Some days he gave me one floor to hide on and some days he gave me one room. Some days he would count to twenty-five and some days he would only count to ten. So many times, I had to play this game with him during the spring of 1981 and it wasn't no game to me. One day I was hiding under my oldest brother's bed in the attic. He came home so I popped out letting him know I was there and telling him not to tell Dave I was hiding. But he hollered down the stairs to let him know he found me.

I bawled my eyes out as Dave escorted me down the attic stairs and into his bedroom. I looked at my brother as I slowly slid down those attic stairs crying, "Why did you tell him?" Dave placed me on the foot of his bed, he unzipped his pants and forced my mouth open. I gagged, cried and kept moving any part of my body I could. He smacked me upside my head and forced my mouth open again. He kept whacking me as he slammed his penis into my mouth. When he felt teeth, I got a whack upside my head again. I kept trying to get away and then we heard a loud click sound. Dave quickly pulled his penis away from me, but he knew he was caught as he quickly went to his bedroom door that opened after my brother knocked on it. That was the loud click we heard; the doorknob clicked when it opened. I quickly jumped up so my brother could see me over Dave's shoulder. I jumped up on the bed, stood up and I saw my brother. I assumed he saw me but it was hard to tell while I had tears pouring down my face. Dave handed him money through the door and when he turned around, he saw me standing on the bed. He grabbed my feet and I was quickly laying on the bed. Then he pulled my arm and made me sit with my legs dangling over the bed. "Ohhhh you think your brother is going to get you help?" Dave laughed as he questioned me. "I'll tell you what," he said as he pulled a cooler of beer, he had on his bedroom floor closer to him. "We will wait," he said before laughing for minutes upon minutes. "You really think your brother is getting you help?" he questioned me again and again. "Yes, he is," I yelled at him, "He saw me," I yelled again as I folded my arms together and cried. Dave laughed, ridiculed and screamed in my face, "No one cares about you." He laughed as he poked me on my head and then did to me what he has been doing to me my whole childhood. He viciously attacked me that day after we waited for help to arrive that never did. He had to carry me back to my bed after he was done with me as my body just slumped onto the floor. When my mother came home, she found me in my bed and she wanted to know why I peed on her bed. I cried and told her what happened, but as I talked, she walked out my bedroom door as she had done hundreds of times before. A few hours later I went downstairs and there was a sign hanging on the basketball hoop right outside the front door. "Mom," I screamed as I pointed to what I could see hanging outside. It was a degrading sex act with my name on it written in black marker. My mother quickly called my oldest brother inside and yelled at him to take it down. My brother didn't get me help that day but he did write a sign about what he saw. The sign read, 'Cathy gives head.' Didn't my brother know I was only eleven years old?

One Saturday I ran up to my bedroom to grab my skateboard before my mother left for work. I told my mother I'd be right back. She said she'd wait for me but when I ran out of my bedroom with my skateboard in hand, I slammed right into Dave who was standing outside my doorway. My skateboard went flying out of my hand as the impact caused me to bounce back and fall down onto the floor. "You have one room today, your bedroom," he said looking down at me with a smile on his face. I quickly jumped up and yelled for my mother, but she was already gone. I begged, "No please." But he said over my voice, "I'll count to fifteen," and he started to count. He blocked my doorway so I couldn't leave.

I turned around, looked at my bed and at my closet, but he always found me there. I ran to my bedroom window, I opened it and jumped out. I didn't care where I landed or what bone I would break, anything was better than being in arm's length of Dave. I landed on the rooftop of the back door porch. I quickly turned to the window I just jumped out and I saw Dave reaching his arm out to me as he tried grabbing me. I moved away a little as I was afraid of falling off but I also was afraid of Dave reaching

1975-1982 Lowell Massachusetts

me. I moved to the furthest corner of the rooftop as Dave continued trying to grab me, when suddenly we both heard something. I looked over to our neighbor's backyard (the one with the greener grass) and there was the neighbor working in his garden. Dave put his finger to his mouth and quietly said, "Shhhhh." Because I was on the rooftop of the porch and the neighbor was into his gardening, Dave knew he didn't see or hear us up on the second floor. That was when I hollered downward, "Hi Mr. Jarek." He looked up, told me to be careful and went back to his gardening. I looked and saw Dave hiding away from the window so the neighbor didn't see him.

I sat on that back porch rooftop from about four in the afternoon until my mother got home from work after nine o'clock. At one point Dave and both my brothers were in the backyard trying to convince me to come down, but I stayed until I saw my mother's face in my bedroom window. "What are you doing out there?" my mother questioned me. "Because of your boyfriend," I screamed at my mother. "He's not stopping until he kills me," I told my mother but she didn't care. I then wrote her a letter about why I wanted to live. I wrote how Dave said he was killing me by the time I was twelve years old. I wrote how I wanted to live and I wrote how I wanted her to have him arrested. I signed it, 'Please mom I want to live, your other daughter Cathy.' I folded it up into a triangle and I handed it to her while she was in her bedroom. I was a lost soul. My own mother would tease, ridicule and belittle me all the time. She would make fun of me for thinking someone would help me from Dave. "Come on huh what would he want with a kid," she would tell me. Then she would threaten me, "You shut your mouth about it." After I'd remind her that she's known since Fletcher Street, she would show her lack of support, "I'll tell them you're lying," she snapped with a smirk on her face. With an extra stupid smirk on her face, she continued with her lack of support and say, "No one will believe you anyways." And if I stayed standing in front of her longer, she would say for me, "To just forget about it ok?" Then I would run up to my bedroom and cry.

Dave was constantly choking me into blackouts, hocking his spit into my face and fully using me at his disposal. Over six years of viciously sexually, physically, terrorizing and traumatizing my childhood. He got joy out of what he was doing to me. He would bounce in his own excitement, laugh at his own joy and smile as he praised about his progress, he has made in all his years with me. He would lecture me to be thankful towards him because, "I let you live an extra couple of years," he hollered in my face. "Sure, was a lot of fun, right?" he continued to say as no matter what I answered, it was the wrong answer each time. I lived in a house where I believed I was nothing more than worthless.

I had nothing, no self-esteem, no love at home, no safety net and I slept with one eye open. I slept with pens, pencils, Barbie dolls, marbles and other toys I could use as weapons when Dave came into my room at nighttime. I would sneak around doorways or the stairs to make sure I didn't cross Dave's path. I continued double tying my shoelaces, wearing extra shirts and pants with sweatpants. I continued to beg, plead, question, remind and hound my mother to make Dave stop abusing me. But nothing could have prepared me for the last and final attack I would suffer in the hands of my mother's boyfriend, Dave Umpleby up in the attic of Pleasant Street in early spring 1981.

It was the Saturday after Easter Sunday of 1981; I woke up hearing my mother getting ready for work. "You told me you weren't working," I said to my mother with a confused look on my face as I jumped out of bed before fully waking up. She snapped at me, "I got called in." I quickly pleaded with her, "Please wait for me to get dressed?" She responded, "Hurry up." I booked it upstairs into my bedroom and I changed my pajamas into clothes quicker than superman in a phone booth. Then I booked it out of my bedroom and smack dab into Dave. I ran right into him, stopped myself from falling and yelled in a bratty voice, "Leave me alone," as I attempted to go around him. But he blocked me with one of his arms "Mom," I yelled down the stairs. "Leave me alone, my mother's downstairs," I snapped at Dave as if he was the one getting in trouble. "She left already," he said as he blocked the stairs in the upstairs hallway, preventing me from going down them.

"I'll give you two floors," he said to me as I instantly started to cry and pleaded to him, "Please no," I begged him to stop even before he started but he just went on playing his fun game. "I'll count to twenty-five," he told me as he started to count, "One, two, three, four," and I had no choice but to run out of his sight or be viciously raped by him again. So I booked it up the attic stairs, into the playroom that was just cleaned spotless by my brothers and I, days earlier. I knew he was going to come up looking for me as soon as he finished counting. I looked all around the attic playroom and I decided to hide in the playroom closet. It was a wide closet with a slanted roof, small door frame and no door. I closed my eyes and whispered to myself, 'Please no, please no,' over and over again. I prayed to myself until I heard him, "Ohhhhhh Cathy," he yelled in a low voice tone while standing in the middle of the playroom. I was behind the closet door frame; I could see him as I peeked from hockey sticks that were resting against the wall in the dark closet. I kept quietly praying, 'Please not again.' He yelled, "Little girls like you disappear," "Come on out," "You knew this was coming," "Ohhhh Cathy," Dave continued to yell throughout the playroom of the attic as I stayed hiding, trying my hardest not to even breathe. "I got to go check on your sister," he said before letting another holler out, "I know you're in your brother's room," "I'll be back," he warned me. I heard him go down the attic stairs but I didn't dare move. He didn't see me yet and he was going into my brother's bedroom when he came back up so I knew I was safe. I stayed there for a while. I heard him come back upstairs as he went into my brother's bedroom. I heard him hollering and then he was back inside the playroom, standing in the middle of the room.

"Ohhhh Cathy," he yelled again. "Come out and play," he continued to yell throughout the playroom like he was in the 1979 movie Warriors. "Got to go check on your sister again," he hollered out, "I'll be back," he said again as he headed down the attic stairs. I knew he'd be checking the playroom closet next, so I tiptoed out of the closet and into the attic hallway. I thought about running down the two flights of stairs and out the front door but I was afraid Dave would catch me. So, I ran into my brother's bedroom and slid under his bed. He had sleeping bags under there and I moved them, smooshing myself furthest up to the corner wall and using the sleeping bags as a shield. I got mad as I laid under my brother's bed hiding from Dave. I was mad that I was hiding, mad that I'd be like this until my mother got home, mad because I was hungry. I had to pee and I was so sick and tired of living in fear. As the morning turned into afternoon, I continued to hear Dave as he ran up and down the attic stairs looking for me and getting angrier as the day went on. At one point he hollered that he had to make lunch for my sister and again letting me know, "I'll be back," as he continued to holler throughout the attic.

After not finding me in the playroom he came back into my brothers' room, taunting me that I would pay for hiding so good. I didn't know where my brothers were. I knew one worked at Notini's warehouse and the other had a newspaper route. I never saw or heard them that morning. I don't know if it would have changed the events of that day, had I seen or heard my brothers that morning, because for years already, it never stopped Dave. I was so petrified. I didn't want Dave to rape, attack, abuse or torture me anymore. I laid under my oldest brother's bed, crying and so very scared. I squished my face into the sleeping bag or my shirt to wipe the tears and mucus from my face. I thought about crawling out from under my brother's bed and just giving up. My stomach started to growl, I was quietly trying to not cry and I was squished against a wall under my oldest brother's bed. But I stayed put as fear overpowered my decision. Dave hollered into the attic hallway each time he had to go down the stairs to check on my baby sister. "I got to go check on your sister," he hollered, then he'd add, "I'll be back." I heard him repeat it all morning and afternoon long. I wouldn't dare move. He didn't find me hiding in my brother's room and I didn't think he'd come back into my brother's bedroom, so I just stayed put. My mother left for work on Saturday mornings around seven o'clock and Dave started his fun game at that time. I knew breakfast and lunch already went by and I knew I had been under my brother's bed for a few hours already. Dave came back up the attic stairs after feeding my baby sister her lunch. There was a lot of screaming, smashing and banging going on in the attic playroom, but I didn't dare move out from under my brother's bed. I was quietly crying; I just wanted my mother home and I just wanted to be anywhere but underneath my brother's bed hiding from Dave. He went downstairs to check on my baby sister a few more times before coming up the attic and losing it. He began yelling louder, screaming louder and demanding that I show my face. "Now," he screamed so loud as he banged and threw things in the attic playroom. "Get out here now," he continued as he yelled, "The woman I made you," "I was going to let you live until your twelve," "Ohhhhhhh Cathy," "Girls like you disappear," he continued yelling along with more smashing and slamming things off the walls.

Then he yelled, "Ok games over, come out, come out wherever you are," he yelled throughout the attic playroom. "I'll count to ten and you better come out from hiding," Dave yelled as he became impatient on finding me. He counted to ten and then laughed an evil laugh until I heard him say, "This is going to be fun." I continued to hear loud banging coming from the playroom. If I squished a part of the sleeping bag a little then I was able to see the floor of my brother's bedroom. I saw the bottom of his bedroom door and the bottom of his closet door. Then I saw Dave's tan work boots walking back into my brother's bedroom. I saw my brother's closet door open; I closed my eyes into the sleeping bags I used as a shield. Then I felt a hard jab into my leg, I bit hard down on the sleeping bag. Dave was using something to poke under my brother's bed. He jabbed my leg bone but I think he thought it was the wall. I really thought he found me when he jammed my leg but he didn't. He went through my brother's closet again and stood in my brother's bedroom for a few before going back to the playroom.

Dave again hollered into the attic hallway, "Got to go check on your sister." As he headed downstairs, he yelled, "And I know you're in your brother's room," "I'll be back," he continued to yell as my eyes widened over hearing him say that. I panicked as I listened to make sure there was no sound. I knew I had to get out of my brother's bedroom because he was coming back in there once he came upstairs again. I knew I had to get out from under my brother's bed. Once I knew it was quiet and safe to do so, I slid out from under my brother's bed. I tiptoed into the hallway, I looked down the stairs and saw the attic door was opened. Knowing Dave was down there, I quietly tiptoed into the playroom. I saw what all the smashing and banging against the wall was, it was Dave making the neatly cleaned playroom into a total mess again.

I ran to the middle of the playroom, looked around and thought to myself, 'Mom's going to be so mad.' I knew she would blame me for the mess, but then I reminded myself to quickly hide as I looked around for a place I could hide. Dave made such a mess of the room as I looked over at the toy box that rested in the far corner of the playroom. I took a look at the attic hallway and knew he would be coming up the stairs, so I made a split decision to run over to the toy box and jump inside. I moved toys as I maneuvered my way inside the toy box and placed toys on top of myself in an attempt to not to be seen. Dave came upstairs and I heard him in my brother's bedroom yelling so loud, banging and demanding, "Show your fucking face," "Now," he screamed. Then he came back into the playroom. Only this time I could smell him when he stood near the toy box. He continued to yell, scream and demand I show my face. He would holler out, "I'll be back," and then pretend to walk down the attic stairs. I could hear him; I could smell him and I knew when he was only pretending to go down the stairs. The attic floors creaked, especially at the top step, that's how I knew he didn't really go downstairs all the times he said he was. But nothing could prevent me from peeing my pants as I laid inside the toy box. I was in that toy box for a long time. I was under my brother's bed for a long time and I was hiding behind the hockey sticks for a long time. As I started to pee, I just let it all come out. I had to pee so bad and there was no holding it in anymore.

As I laid hiding in a toy box, I continued to hear, feel and smell the presence of Dave. The booze that reeked from him, his grunts, huffs and his anger. Dave continued to taunt, yell and scream. He continued to threaten, demand and he continued to pretend to be walking down the attic stairs. I got a really bad leg cramp as I laid squished inside the toy box. I kept telling myself, 'Don't move, don't move.' I must have said it hundreds of times to myself. Dave had to go downstairs to check on my baby sister again. "I'll be back," he hollered again. I waited and I waited until I knew for a fact that Dave really did go downstairs to check on my baby sister. It was quiet, there was no creaking of the floors, no heavy breathing from Dave and no smell of him. So, I knew I was safe to straighten my leg out a bit. I reached my hand through the toys on top of me so I could grab my leg where I was getting the cramp from, then I slowly straightened my leg as much as I could while laying inside of the toy box. As I stretched my leg, I heard a loud noise from Dave. Then I felt a hard yank on my head as I was pulled out of the toy box by my neck and there I was, dangling in the air. Dave was holding me by my throat above him, his face red in anger as he yelled about the trouble, I caused for hiding so well. Then I felt a hard thump as I was slammed onto the attic floor like a football on a winning touchdown. My head and face burned in pain from the contact onto the wooden floor. My legs slammed down like a weight with no landing. But before I could make any sense of it all, Dave kicked me with his work boot. I felt the impact on my mid area as he continued to kick and kick and kick and kick me. At one point I was on top of his work boot but quickly flung off as he began to stomp on my face with his boot. He continued to stomp on me, kick me and stomp and kick until I wasn't feeling the pain of the kicks or stomps anymore. They were more of my body just being thrust upon with each kick and stomp of his work boot. I saw the bottom of his boot as it connected to my jaw and side of my face. But I didn't feel it, I wasn't feeling anything, just the movement of my body with every kick and stomp Dave did to me that day.

I heard a commotion; everything was foggy as I saw a blurry Dave being pulled away from me. He was pulled away by two people but I only saw and heard one, "You ok Cathy?" my older brother questioned me as he kneeled down on the attic floor. I tried looking up at him as I was gasping for breath but I could only see his legs folded sitting next to me. "You better call mom," he said to whoever else was in the room. I must have blacked out for however long it took them to call my mother at her work and for her to drive home from her job at Kings department store in Tewksbury, Mass. "Cathy, Cathy, moms here," I heard my older brother say. I opened my eyes and saw he was still kneeled down next to me on the floor. I moved my eyes to the doorway of the attic and saw my mother coming up the top step into the attic hallway. My mother immediately kneeled down next to me and yelled, "What the heck happened?" she questioned as I spit blood out of my mouth and tried telling her, "I didn't make this mess." My mother cradled me into her arms as I was unable to get up or move. My brother argued with her that he should carry me down the attic stairs, but it was my mother who carried me down the stairs and into my bed. She gave me tissues for the blood in my mouth and nose, then she left my room for a few minutes.

I heard talking in the hallway as my bedroom door wasn't closed all the way. My mother soon came back into my room with scissors, bandages, a bucket of water and face cloths. She cut my clothes off and proceeded to wash me. A couple of back teeth is what caused all the blood inside my mouth as I spit them out onto a cloth my mother was washing my face with. "Jesus Christ," my mother said, "What the heck happened?" she continued. But it hurt to talk and all I could say was, "Why does he hate me?" I questioned as I continued to cough up blood and gasp for breaths. My mother gently washed my battered face with a couple of washcloths. There was so much blood. My mother then wrapped my mid area in a bandage but stopped as I continued to cry in pain. I was then left alone as my mother shut my bedroom door and everything went dark. I cried myself to sleep as I was in so much pain.

I woke up to my mother shoving her ear in my face. "What, ouch, are you, ouch, doing?" I questioned her as I felt an excruciating pain. It hurt to breathe, it hurt to move and it hurt everywhere from my face to my mid area. I could feel the swelling on my face. The way I talked was slurred due to my swollen face. My mother finished wrapping my mid area with bandages and tape. She would bring food and drinks to me in my bed as I healed from my injuries. She would bring my toothbrush, toothpaste and rinsing water in a cup to me in my bed. She would carry a stainless-steel bowl into my room when I had to pee and slide it under my buttocks so

I could pee. She would give me a wash down in my bed and change my clothes for me as I healed from my injuries. One day I had to go poop and after removing my pants, my mother cradled and carried me to the bathroom with a towel over me. She sat me on the toilet and said to me, "Flush so I know when you're done," and, "Don't look in the mirror," she continued. I probably wouldn't have but since she said not to, I thought about it. The bathroom mirror was the medicine cabinet above the bathroom sink. I couldn't reach it and I could barely move. When I was finished instead of flushing, I closed the toilet seat and kneeled on it. My ribs burned in pain, but I managed to swing the mirror door open because it wasn't closed all the way. I stretched my head upwards, got a look at my face and screamed bloody murder. My mother came in, cradled me and carried me back to my bed, yelling at me for disobeying her. My face was deformed and swollen from the injuries I suffered and my neck was red, black and blue. Both my brothers came into my room. My oldest brother said, "Wow he really fucked you up." I just looked at him, "You think?" I answered him as I laid in my bed. "Did someone call the cops on him?" I questioned both my brothers and my mother who was in my room. But my other older brother who was leaning against my dresser bureau said, "You don't call the cops on family." I yelled as loud as I could, "I want the cops called on him." My mother then shooed my brothers out of my bedroom and shut my door when she walked out behind them. I was asking anyone who walked by my open bedroom door to call the police on Dave, then my mother decided to keep my bedroom door closed at all times. A few days later my mother came storming into my bedroom. She flung my bedroom door open, came over to my bed, pulled my blankets off me, lifted my shirt and started ripping the bandages off my mid area. "What are you doing?" I questioned my mother as I cried in an unbearable pain.

She then pulled Dave's polaroid camera from between her legs and started to take pictures of the injuries on my face and mid area. "What are you doing?" I questioned her as I was horrified over what she was doing to me. "So, I can put these with his other freaking trophy photos," my mother snapped at me. She then collected the photos she placed on my bed and said to me, "So he can remember what he did to you every time he looks at them." I was terrified how my mother took photos of the injuries Dave did to me. She was so nasty about it. I don't think my mother was mad because I was injured, it seemed like she was mad because I was visibly injured. The injuries I suffered from Dave that day in the attic was a badly beaten face, loss of teeth, a badly bruised, scraped, scratched and hand burnt neck, black and blue bruises fully on the left side and partial on right side of my mid area, multiple beyond multiple broken ribs and no one called the police on Dave. One day I crawled to my mother's bedroom to use her phone and call the police, but when I pulled the cord to make the phone fall off her bureau, she ran up the stairs and carried me back to my bed. I was unable to attend school as I was unable to get out of bed. I was unable to sit up on my own and I was unable to call the police. It was all I wanted, was someone to call the police. I couldn't move for a few weeks after Dave attacked me in the attic. All I wanted was someone to call the cops on him, but no one did.

My mother continued to bring me food, drinks, coloring books, puzzles, a pan to pee in, a toothbrush with a cup of water and toothpaste to me in my bed as I continued to suffer in pain over the injuries Dave did to me. One morning I awoke to my mother opening my shades in my room. "Time to get up," she hollered throughout my room as the bright sun glared through the window. I tried to slide myself upward when I screamed in pain. "Why does it hurt so much mom?" I questioned her. And it did, I was in so much pain, I hurt all over, I was already in tears and I just woke up. "Of course, it hurts," my mother said, "What do you expect with broken ribs?" she continued. I looked at her and questioned, "Their broken?" She laughed at me as she said, "Of course their broken, just look at your bruises." I immediately told my mother, "You have to take me to the hospital." But my mother laughed at me again and insisted that hospitals don't do anything for broken ribs because they heal on their own.

While my mother changed the bandages on my mid area one day, I screamed in horror asking her, "Who colored on me?" as I looked at the black skin on my chest and stomach. It was a huge bruise that looked like a black marker had been colored on me. Because my door remained closed for so long, it was a while before I saw Dave walk by my open bedroom door and I was devastated to know he was still living with us. I was stuck in my room for over three weeks and as I gradually healed, my mother would gradually defend Dave even though half my mid area was black, blue, yellow, green and brown, she defended Dave. I was so mad at my mother when I realized Dave was still living in the house. "Why is he still here?" I yelled at my mother. I wanted her to call the cops on Dave but she insisted he was embarrassed by the whole ordeal because now, "Everybody in the house knows what he did to you." Those were her motherly words to me.

I questioned my mother to call the police, I pleaded to my mother to call the police, I hounded my mother to call the police and I begged my mother to call the police on Dave, but she never did. One day my mother came charging into my room, "Shh stay quiet," she told me. "He's coming home for lunch," she continued. "He's not in a good mood," she warned me. "I'll tell him you're sleeping," she quickly informed me about Dave coming home for lunch. I heard the front door when he came home and I heard my mother talking and laughing downstairs with him. I didn't dare make a sound. I just laid in my bed trying to figure out why he still lived with us. I heard the front door again and shortly afterwards my mother came into my bedroom. "Here," she said as she handed me a stack of school papers. "What's this?" I questioned her and she answered me, "Your school work." I was totally confused. "Where did you get this?" I questioned her. She snapped at me, "From your teacher," as she continued, "She just dropped it off." Again, I was confused, "But you said Dave was coming home for lunch," I said to my mother. With a straight face my mother said to me, "No I only said that because you have a big mouth." I looked at my mother and I again begged her, pleading with her, "Mom please call the cops on him." But what I was saying to her went in one ear and straight out the other. My mother wanted me, "To think about forgiving Dave," she suggested one day. "Mom please," I started to say as she cut me off to tell me, "He is sorry for hurting you," "He is embarrassed over it," she continued as I continued defending myself. "Mom he's raping me," I told her. "Mom he's going to kill me," I continued repeating while my mother talked louder over me. So, I talked louder over her, "He's raping me," "He's raping me," I continued repeating until, 'SLAP.' My mother slapped me right across my face and stormed out of my bedroom. I thought to myself, 'Like I'm not hurting enough, you had to slap me?'

My mother continued her unmotherly care on me as I healed in my bed from injuries caused by Dave. She was the most genuine to me when she would sit on my bed and explain to me how sorry Dave was for hurting me and she wanted me to give him a chance to come into my room and apologize to me. I yelled, "No," at my mother as she told me, "Just think about it." She continued to hound me about forgiving him, about letting him inside my bedroom so he could apologize as I healed in my bed from the injuries he caused. My mother started to buy me things, new clothes, a record player, crafts and more. But I knew why she was doing it and I'd remind her every time, "I'm not forgiving your boyfriend," and, "He's not touching me again." But like so many times before, my mother just walked out of my bedroom. One day she came charging in my bedroom, "This is going to end today," she declared as she stormed into my room. I looked up and there was my mother with Dave standing on the side of her. "You are going to listen to him apologize," she told me and being stuck in my bed for weeks already, I had no choice but to listen to Dave apologize for kicking the shit out of me. He apologized for hurting me and for scaring me. He told me how he didn't mean to hurt me and how it would mean a lot to him if I accepted his apology. I looked back and forth to my mother and Dave many, many times as I laid in my bed, throbbing in pain and listening to these adults before me. "Well Cathy," my mother said to me.

"Do you accept his apology?" she questioned. She then let me know, "How nice he just was by apologizing to you," she said with a smile. They stood before me waiting for me to accept his apology. "Well Cathy, do you?" my mother questioned me again and with all my might and all my strength, I screamed out the word, "No," right up to their faces and it pissed my mother off.

As I continued to heal in my bedroom, my mother continued to defend

Dave. I worked on my big stack of school papers which kept me busy while I was confined to my bed. As I gradually started moving and walking around my room, I also started to find ways to get help. My mother caught me yelling out my window to my neighbor and she put nails on the window so I couldn't open it anymore. My mother caught me writing the letters SOS on my window in chalk and erased it. I would switch my bedroom light on and off every time I heard or saw the flashing lights of an airplane flying over the skies. I truly believed the pilot would be able to see my light. My mother cut the string on my bedroom light so I couldn't reach it anymore. I'm sure she knew the people in the airplane couldn't see my bedroom light and she still cut the string.

I started to walk around the home and would go downstairs when Dave wasn't home. It hurt to make it down the stairs at first. My mother was turning my school work in to the school and returning with more school work for me to do. I was finally getting good grades back from my returned school work. Maybe it was because Dave hadn't bothered me since the attack in the attic and I was finally able to concentrate on my school work rather than where I was hiding next from Dave. As I was moving around more, my black and blue bruises were now in greens, yellows and browns. I had not been outside or seen any of my friends since I was attacked in the attic weeks earlier. I was walking on eggshells, afraid of each and every move I made in that house. As I started to feel better, walking around more, up and down the stairs more, I'd question my mother when I would be able to go back to school and I would have to raise my shirt to see how my bruises looked before she would answer me. Finally, I was able to go out, it was to a barbecue pool party at my mother's sister's house. It was Memorial Day weekend 1981 and I was told we all had to go. "Wait me to?" I excitedly questioned my mother. She told me to grab my bathing suit and she insisted I bring a long t-shirt. I went up to my room, still unable to run. I grabbed my new bathing suit my mother gave me in a bribery attempt to forgive Dave. But I purposely forgot the long t-shirt which I did own a couple of. When I got back downstairs everyone was heading out the front door. My mother grabbed my goggles and bathing suit as she stuffed it in a bag while trying to rush me out the door. "Ouch," I yelled in pain as my mother attempted to push me faster. Then I stopped in my tracks, "Why is he coming?" I questioned my mother as Dave grabbed the car keys from her hand and headed out the door. "Because you have a big mouth," my mother said to me. "Oh my God mom," I cried to her, "You're letting him hurt me," I cried as we walked out the door and got into the back seat of my mother's car. Dave drove as I sunk down so he couldn't see me in the rearview mirror. Once at my aunt's home there were a good amount of people there, everyone was having fun. I was a very quiet kid and I mean an extremely quiet kid. Not because I wanted to but because I was just trained to be.

"Where's your t-shirt?" my mother questioned me as she pulled my stuff out of the bag. "Ha-ha oops," I said to my mother with a smirk. My mother leaned into me and told me not to go in the pool, "Tell them you don't feel good if anyone asks," she said as I just looked at my mother and rolled my eyes. It wasn't long until my aunt questioned me about going in the pool. I then looked at my mother, "Mom you got my bathing suit?" I questioned her. That gave me a dirty look from my mother. She took me into the bathroom and tried covering my bruises with makeup, but it didn't work. She left the bathroom and came back with Dave's t-shirt and made me wear it. I was shy, but I was also scared. I waited until the pool didn't have as many kids in it. All the older kids got out to eat and I climbed up the ladder and slowly climbed into the pool. I wasn't in the pool but for a few minutes when I saw him heading towards the pool. It was Dave and I froze. I watched him walk to the pool, I watched him climb the ladder and I watched him dive in. He swam around the shape of the pool and brushed against me. It was the first time that man touched me since he attacked me in the attic. I know he only brushed against me but I let out a holy horror scream and whatever adult was on the outside of the pool, pulled me out of the pool from where he was standing. And every single adult was looking at the commotion going on. As I was lifted out of the pool my aunt saw my bruises and yelled at my mother. Then there was so much yelling as my mother dragged me out of the yard and into her car. It was hot out, hot in my mother's car and I was bawling my eyes out. Then my brothers joined me in the car. Not long after my mother and Dave appeared from my aunt's yard. We all headed home where I was grounded again. "For causing trouble at the cookout," my mother said was the reason why I was grounded. 'Grounded,' I thought to myself. I have been confined to my room for weeks, I was in extreme pain for weeks, I was still recovering from my injuries, I still had bruises, I still had painful ribs, I couldn't run, I couldn't defend myself and I was grounded. I barely came out of my room that week.

I thought a real lot about all the times I went to my mother about Dave. From Fletcher Street to Pleasant Street to Wyman's beach and back. 'She's not stopping him,' I began to realize. I thought a real lot about my brothers and all those knocks on the bedroom door, all the times they were home, the attack I suffered in the attic and no one called the police. I was baffled, I was beyond myself, I was helpless and I was hopeless. Dave started coming into my room at night time again. "I'm not going to hurt you," he'd say over and over again as he walked towards my bed insisting, he just wanted to talk. "Glad I didn't hurt your arms," he'd say to me as he rubbed the tip of his finger down my arm. I'd try to move away, scream or beg him to go away. He would just come in the next night and do the same as he fantasized over my arms. "Oh, I'm keeping these as souvenirs," he'd say so happily. "Sooooo pretty," he continued to taunt me as he rubbed his fingers along my arms, telling me in a nicely manner, "You know your mother is stupid," he'd say as he laughed while he talked. "I have her wrapped around my finger," he told me. I started sleeping with marbles I took from my brother and throwing them at Dave when he came into my bedroom. I got him one night, right in the face.

He immediately headed back out of my bedroom and I knew I was in trouble. My mother took away all the marbles. I was left sleeping with whatever pen, pencil or toy I could use as a weapon when Dave came into my room. Finally at the end of the week my mother told me I would be going back to school on Monday as I was about to graduate from the 6th grade in a few weeks. She also said she would allow me to go outside over the weekend. It was a nice Friday afternoon and I was super excited over the news my mother told me, so I decided to leave my bedroom and head downstairs to ask my mother if I could go outside. I walked through the downstairs hallway and into the kitchen. Dave was washing his hands at the kitchen sink and saw me at the doorway of the kitchen and hall. I immediately turned to walk away when he questioned, "You looking for your mother?" I turned around, nodded my head as I said, "Yes." "She's down in the cellar," he said to me as he kicked at the open cellar door. I leaned into the doorway of the cellar and hollered down the stairs, "Mom you down there?" I had not been in the cellar since Dave last dragged me down there. So, I was a bit cautious at what he had to say. But then my mother hollered back up the cellar stairs, "Yup I'm down here." I immediately headed down there with the intentions to ask my mother if I could go outside for a little while before it got dark.

WHEN I got to the bottom of the cellar stairs, my mother was standing straight across the cellar, looking over a huge pile of rocks and stone. I walked over to where she was, "What are you, what the heck," I said as I looked at my mother confused, "What are you doing?" I questioned, "And what is this?" I continued to question my mother. "I'm getting rocks for the garden," my mother said to me. I looked at her strangely. "What garden?" I questioned her. "We haven't had one in years," I continued saying to my mother when I suddenly froze. Dave was now down in the cellar. He came down the stairs and walked behind me so he was now standing to the left of me. I looked at my mother beyond confused as she moved to the right of me. Dave questioned my mother, "Did you show her yet?" I looked at my mother, "Show me what?" I questioned her. I was looking at my mother in total confusion, waiting for her to answer me. I looked at Dave then back at my mother, then I looked at what they were both looking at. A huge, well dug out hole going right through the wall and into the sidewalk below Pleasant Street. Dave had a broom and dustpan he was using to sweep the inside of the hole in the wall. I looked at my mother confused as Dave started talking. "This is your punishment for having a big mouth," he said to me. I looked at him as he continued talking. "Jump in, try it out," he said as if he was finding pride in what he had accomplished. I looked at my mother in beyond total confusion and she tried clearing my confusion up as she said to me, "Cathy what he is trying to say is you don't need to go blabbing to your friends what goes on in this house." Then Dave continued, "Don't worry someone will find you in twenty or thirty years," he said with a laugh, "Your arms will be here waiting," he continued. I just looked at Dave with huge eyes as my mother snapped at him, "You can't scare her like that." They bickered back and forth. I used the opportunity to run up the cellar stairs. My ribs were still sore, but I booked it up the stairs fast. I was going to run right out the front door but it was closed and locked.

I saw my baby sister alone in her closed-in play area in the living room, so I went to sit with her. I was playing with her when my mother came behind me and said, "Cathy, he won't really put you in there," "He was only trying to give you a scare," she continued. "Ya right, you let him chain me down there," I yelled at her just as I saw Dave standing behind her and knowing he heard me, I ran up to my bedroom. My mother came in to check on me before bed and we got into a huge fight about Dave. I stayed awake the whole night. I sat on my bed surrounding myself with whatever I could throw at Dave when he came into my bedroom. Pens, dolls, barrettes, shoes, flip flops, anything my mother didn't take away from me. Then Dave came into my room and I threw them one at a time. "Please just leave me alone," I begged him. But he didn't care, no one cared. Dave returned the same two sex toys to me that night after everything I had was thrown at him. He insisted I needed to practice, "We have a lot of catching up to do," he said to me as I cried to him, "Please just leave me alone." I screamed for my mother and not once did she come to my room. After Dave left my room, I flung the sex toys away from me, dragged my bureau to my bedroom door and got dressed. Putting on clothes, shoes and then I sat on my bed. I did a lot of thinking, crying and more thinking.

A Childhood Tragedy Under a Mother's Watch

So many thoughts went through my head that night. I thought about when my mother insisted, I started my period years earlier. I told her it was from Dave hurting me but no matter how many times I told her that I didn't start my period, she insisted the blood on my underwear was not from Dave hurting me. I tried to understand how or why my mother was still defending a man who had been terrorizing me for years and then I thought of my brothers. I wondered, what did they hear on the other side of my mothers and Dave's bedroom door for all these years? Then I thought about all the times a brother would knock on the bedroom door and how Dave would open it a little. I tried to yell or be seen by them before Dave would quickly shut the door. Did they ever wonder what was happening to me inside that room? I thought about the times I would grab onto a doorway or the banister to the stairs tightly as Dave carried me away, causing him to have a hard time and asking whoever was walking by to release my hands. I thought about all the times I screamed as Dave carried me to his bedroom, all the times I cried, all the times I fought to not be assaulted and still no one in that home helped or protected me from Dave. I thought about all the times my mother yelled, slapped or degraded me for telling her about Dave. I thought about the people who questioned my fear of Dave throughout the years but didn't act on it. I thought about the film projector I told my mother about. The camcorder I told her about. I thought about the attack that I was still healing from and how no one called the cops on a man who almost killed me that day in the attic. I thought about how I believed it was normal to live in a world where all families had secrets, where it was the child who was looked down upon for being abused. I thought about all the times I told my mother how Dave made me smell a cloth and it made me fall asleep. I thought about all the times I told my mother about Dave, all the times she was home on Fletcher Street and all the times my brothers and mother were home on Pleasant Street. I felt so unloved and unwanted.

Now there was a hole dug into the wall down in the cellar and I was supposed to believe that Dave wasn't going to hurt me anymore because my mother insisted, "Everyone in the house knows what he did to me." So many thoughts went through my head. I thought about running away, I

1975-1982 Lowell Massachusetts

looked out my window and thought to myself, 'where would I go?' I fell asleep sitting up in bed until I awoke to my bureau being dragged and my door slowly opening. "Get out," I yelled. My mother poked her hand in, waved it and said, "It's only me." I immediately said to my mother, "Mom he came in my room again," "Look," I continued as I pointed to the sex toys on the end of my bed. She grabbed them from my bed and then said to me, "Just stay in your room today." I was about to question her why but she continued, "I got called into work." I went into instant alert mode, "Wait, what, no," I pleaded. "No," I yelled, "I am not staying home with him," I screamed as I chased my mother out of my bedroom, down the stairs and straight out the front door. Thank God I was already dressed, had I wasted time getting dressed, Dave probably would have caught me. I yelled at my mother from the sidewalk, "I'm not staying with your boyfriend ever again." All my mother did was yell at me to get back in the house. At one point she stepped out of her car to slap me back into the house, but I was too quick for her and moved out of her reach. She then hopped back in her car and drove away as I continued to beg her, "Please don't leave me with him." But she did, I watched as she drove away, then I turned and looked at the front door to my home and thought to myself, 'No way.'

I already knew I couldn't knock on one of my friend's doors so early in the morning, but my new friend a few houses down, meant I was further away from my house. So, I ran to her house which was on the opposite side of the street. I climbed the front steps, knocked and rang the doorbell. Her mother answered in her pajamas and robe. She told me everyone was still sleeping and for me to come back later. "I'll wait here on the porch," I said to her. Moments later my friend came to the door and invited me inside. She went back to bed and I zonked out on their living room sofa, knowing I was safe. After everyone was awake, we ate breakfast and I played Barbie dolls in my friend's bedroom.

Her mom came into the bedroom in mid-morning asking if I could do her a favor. I immediately jumped up and agreed. Then the smile was wiped off my face as she questioned me to go get a couple of cigarettes from my mother's boyfriend. "I already called him," she said to me. My face expression caused concern to my friend's mother. "What is going on over there?" she questioned me, but I just looked down to the floor. My friend's mother insisted she would watch me the whole way and wait for me on her porch. So, I walked to my house as my friend's mother watched from her porch. I went inside to retrieve the cigarettes from Dave and left the front door open. "Shut the door," Dave said to me as he sat in his recliner chair with a few cigarettes sticking out of his hand. I pleaded with him, "Come on please," but he just kept demanding I shut the door. "And then I'll give you the cigarettes," he said in a perky manner as he continued sitting in his chair with his arm stretched out, holding the cigarettes and waving them at me. After going back and forth with him, I slowly shut the door. Just as quickly Dave jumped from his recliner, "I'll bring her the cigarettes," he said as he began to charge at me.

If I opened the door, he would have grabbed me, so I quickly ran. "Someone is going down cellar," he said as I booked it down the hallway and through the dining room. He caught me by my legs as I ran through the living room and we both fell. I kicked and kicked my legs and then I heard, "Ouch you bitch." The grip of his hands let go of my legs, I looked at him and saw I either kicked him in his jaw or he bit his tongue. I immediately jumped up, ran out the front door, booked it to my friend's house, up her front steps and right into my friend who was standing with her mom on their porch.

"I couldn't get the cigarettes," I said to my friend's mother. But she wasn't worried about the cigarettes, she was worried about me. We went back inside their home where I continued to play with my friend. My friend's mother told me shortly afterwards that she had called my mother at her work and informed me that I was going to stay with them until my mother got out of work.

Later in the afternoon my friend's mother told me my mother was home. "You come back here if you have to, ok?" my friend's mother said to me before I left. As I got to my house my mother was outside by her car. "I'm not going inside that house if he's in there," I said to my mother. "Get in the car," she snapped at me as she got in the driver's side of her car. I got in her car and questioned her, "Where are we going?" My mother answered my question with a question, "What the heck did you say to her?" I looked at her confused, "Say to who?" I snapped back at her. "Your friends' mother," she answered. "She called me at work," my mother continued in a disgusted tone. "Oh her?" I questioned, "I told her everything," I snapped at her with a smirk on my face. Even though I told my friend's mother nothing at all, I wanted my mother to think that I did. The rest of the ride went quiet. "Where are we going?" I questioned my mother again as she pulled the car over and parked. She told me, "I have to stop at my cousins for a minute." We got out of the car and walked inside her cousin Terri's house, the one with the above ground pool my mother would sometimes bring us to. Terri's two teenage daughters were home and I went up to their bedroom to hang out for a few.

I had a lot going on in my head and I wanted to see what my mother was up to. I headed back downstairs to the kitchen where I left my mother and her cousin Terri when I first got there just a few minutes earlier. "Where's my mother?" I questioned Terri. She looked at me and said, "She left, didn't she tell you?" I looked at my mother's cousin a bit confused, "No," I answered her. She looked down at a green trash bag on her kitchen floor, "You're going to stay here for a couple weeks," she informed me. "Didn't your mother tell you?" She questioned me again. I looked at the green trash bag on the floor, looked back up at Terri and said, "No she didn't tell me."

Three
A Family She Never Had

My mother's cousin informed me I would be staying with her and her family for two weeks. I immediately questioned Terri. "What about my graduation?" But she didn't know anything about it. She assumed I would be back home for my 6th grade graduation which was being held in two weeks. I carried my green trash bag of clothes up to the bedroom the two sisters shared. They rolled a mattress on wheels into their room and were super cool towards me. They knew I was upset about the way my mother just left me there. They talked to me about it for a bit. They had a good relationship with their mother and as they talked to me about my mother, I told them, "She's mean to me all the time." They got me a plastic bin for my clothes so I could take them out of the green trash bag they were in. During the time on Pleasant Street while I healed from the physical injuries Dave caused, my mother would continue to spoil me with many things including clothes. I got two new bathing suits, flip flops, sneakers, many summer outfits, pajamas and a beach towel. Not one article of new clothing, shoes or beach towel were inside that green trash bag full of winter clothes.

It was June 1981 and my mother not only abandoned me at her cousin's house but she also left me with no clothes to wear. Lucky for me the two sisters had many bags of hand me down clothing. They were able to find me shorts, tank tops and bathing suits so I could swim in their above ground pool. I had a couple of bad nightmares and the sisters were really cool towards me about it. I was told how I would wake them up from screams and they wanted me to know I was safe sleeping there, "We are right here," as they assured me, I wasn't alone in the bedroom. I called my mother after a day or two. As soon as she answered the phone, I told her it was me on the phone and then questioned her, "Why did you leave without telling me?" With no response, I questioned her again, "Why'd you leave me here?" I was so mad at my mother and her answers only made me angrier at her.

She went on telling me how I was a crybaby, she didn't want me to cry and telling me, "You cause too much trouble at home." As I was defending myself my mother hung up the phone. The two sisters kept me pretty busy, we went swimming a lot, hang around outside in their backyard till late at night or walked to the Sears department store Plaza on Plain Street. We walked around the big parking lot, looking through all the store windows and stopping for an ice cream at Brigham's ice cream shop at the far end of the Plaza. The sisters didn't mind me tagging along with them as we walked around Main, W London, Tanner and Canada streets of a neighborhood in Lowell. We went swimming in their above ground pool, went to their friend's house or stayed up late in their bedroom playing cards.

When the two weeks came around, I called my mother again. "Mom come get me, my graduation is this week," I said to her as soon as she answered, but she hung up. I called her back, the phone picked up and hung up. I called again and same thing, she hung up. The last time I called that day, the phone was giving me the beeping sound of a busy signal. I was so hurt, I felt ashamed, humiliated, an empty hollow tug of my heart. I didn't know what I did that was so wrong or why my mother just left me at her cousin's house. I already missed out on so much thanks to my mother and now I was losing out on attending my 6th grade graduation. I continued to call my mother every day and as my graduation day came, it also went. My mother never called me and she would hang up on me when I called.

As the two weeks came and went, the sisters went away for a planned weekend getaway, leaving me at the home with only my mother's cousin Terri. "Have you heard from your mother?" she questioned me one day and I answered her, "My mother never calls me, hangs up on me or never answers when I call her." She told me there was a phone on the end table and to give my mother a call. When my mother answered, I immediately questioned her, "When are you coming to get me?" and, "Is Dave still there?" She answered in a sarcastic tone, "I'm not and of course he is still here, why wouldn't he be?" she continued answering my questions with questions. I continued to bombard her with more questions, "When are you coming to get me?" "When can I come home?" "Why is he still there?" I started to cry and yell at my mother on the phone about being punished for not wanting Dave to hurt me. My mother's voice on the other end of the phone was answering me the same answers, "No I'm not coming to get you," and, "This is his home too," my mother continued to speak. I was yelling at her, "So because I didn't want to be abused by your boyfriend anymore, I get abandoned," "Why are you doing this mom?" I was sobbing into the phone when I was reminded my mother's cousin was in the room. "Let me talk to your mother," she said to me. Terri heard the whole phone call. I turned around embarrassed knowing she heard all I said, but before I could give her the phone, my mother already hung up her end of the telephone.

"Go to the bathroom and wash your face honey," Terri said to me. I cried more in the bathroom, blew my nose, washed my face and went back into the living room where Terri was still sitting. I sat on the couch, being quiet and watching a television show she was watching. I was feeling a bit awkward when out of the blue I heard her say, "Want to bake some cookies?" Terri questioned me as we jumped up and went in the kitchen where she showed me how to make a batch of homemade chocolate chip cookies. Terri let me know my mother had no clue she was sitting next to me during that whole phone conversation and how my mother said it was a different reason why I was there. She informed me, "Your mother said you were a troublemaker and causing a lot of problems at home," she said as she continued, "But I don't believe her." She explained I was also allowed to stay there for the summer as long as I behaved.

We talked a bit more about my mother but we didn't talk about her boyfriend Dave. When the sisters returned, I went back to swimming, walking around the neighborhood and hanging at their friend's house. The two weeks I was supposed to stay turned into two months as my mother continued to ignore the phone calls from her cousin and her own daughter. I spent the summer of 1981 with two teenagers, like an eleven-year-old having Bill Murray as a camp counselor in the movie Meatballs, I learned a lot and I had a lot of fun.

I had my moments during the summer. Missing my graduation really bummed me out. Missing my older brother's birthday in June really bummed me out and missing my baby sister's birthday in August really bummed me out. The sisters talked with me about Dave and though I would say it was because of him why I wasn't home, I didn't dare talk about the sexual abuse because I was ashamed and embarrassed. I questioned myself over and over again, 'What did I do that was so wrong?' I didn't understand it, but what I did understand was that I wasn't being touched, terrorized, raped or abused by Dave anymore. And that was such a huge load of relief off of my eleven-year-old self. At times I felt like a poor kid with no family and no clothes of my own. I would suck it up when my eyes would swell in tears or when I'd get sad. I hated the way I was looked at sometimes. I would soon know that look to be what it is called, 'A look of pity.' I was included in cleaning chores while I was there, made money off the sisters by doing their chores and I ate dinner with the family every night. I still tried calling my mother in hopes she would answer. She ignored her cousin when she called and she was still ignoring or hanging up on me when I called. I went swimming a lot in the pool and spent most of the summer swimming in it. There were rules to abide by in the home and pool area. One rule was, 'No swimming in the rain.'

While Terri was out one afternoon in late August, we all went swimming even though it was raining out. Terri returned sooner than she said she would and we were all busted swimming in the pool and she was very upset. She yelled at her daughters. She told me, "Get your stuff, you're going home." I went upstairs, got my stuff together as we all giggled upstairs in the bedroom the sisters shared. I was given a duffle bag so I didn't have to put my new hand me down clothes in a trash bag. I thanked them for putting up with me and told them, "I had a lot of fun." On the ride back to my home on Pleasant Street I questioned Terri, "Does my mother know I'm coming?" She informed me she tried calling my mother all summer long and she never answered. I thanked her for letting me stay at her home and apologized for swimming in the rain. As she drove, she told me, "Look you're a good kid." She explained how she didn't understand why my mother did what she did and she was only returning me to my mother because, "Well she's your mother and it's how it goes," she said to me as we turned onto Pleasant Street.

When we pulled up to my home, my mother was standing outside on the porch and it didn't look like she was expecting me at all. Her face dropped when she spotted us. She walked over to Terri's driver's side and I quickly jumped out of the car, grabbed my duffle bag and immediately headed to the front steps of my home. I couldn't wait to run up to my bedroom and see all my books, papers, toys and stuff my father gave me as Christmas gifts the previous holiday. With all the winter clothes my mother tossed in a green trash bag, she never put the pink sweater my dad gave me in it. I just assumed it was in my dresser drawer at home with all my new summer clothes I never got to wear. But I was stopped in my tracks by the time I was on the second front step. I stopped really quick when I saw Dave's feet at his chair through the opened screened front door. I turned to my mother who was in the street talking to her cousin. "Why is he here?" I yelled to my mother as I backed away from the front steps. I put my bag down and turned to question my mother again, "Why is he here?" I yelled as I ran over to my mother, but she quickly rushed me back away from Terri's car and hollered at me to go call my friend Sandi, the one whose house I ran to just a few months earlier. "She's been calling all summer," my mother said to me. I started to run towards where my friend lived when I heard, "She moved, she moved," my mother yelled to me so I would stop running. "What, when?" I questioned my mother as I was really bummed to know she moved. My mother said goodbye to her cousin and told me she had to get Sandi's new phone number inside the house. My only concern as I informed my mother was, "I'm not going in there with him there," as I continued, "Why is he still here?" I questioned in anger. My mother ignored me and ran inside to get my friend Sandi's phone number. I remained outside my home, too afraid to go in with Dave there.

My mother came back outside telling me all I had to do was be quiet as she told me, "He's sleeping, he hasn't seen you yet." She had a piece of paper and pen which she handed to me. "He doesn't know you're here," she told me, "Just go in quietly straight to the kitchen, call your friend and ask if you can sleep over," my mother continued. My heart was smashed all over the sidewalk I stood on as I realized my mother didn't want me there because she wanted her boyfriend there instead. I was flabbergasted and I didn't even know what that word meant.

I felt insulted as I snuck into my home, tiptoeing down the hall and into the kitchen where I called my friend. I kept looking to make sure Dave didn't come into the room while I was on the phone. My friend moved over the summer to the south Lowell area and gave me the address after her mom said I could sleep over if my mother drove me there. I hung up the phone and headed to the front door just as Dave appeared at the doorway of the living room and front hall. He saw me and charged at me but my mother and brothers blocked him as my mother yelled at me to get out the door. I booked it out the door and onto the street where I stood by the passenger side of my mother's car. "Get in," my mother hollered at me as she ran down the outside steps and into her car. "Did she give you

A Childhood Tragedy Under a Mother's Watch

the address?" my mother questioned me as she started her car. I handed her the piece of paper and pen she gave me and said to her, "Yes she said I could sleep over too." I gave her a weird dirty look as I told her the address my friend gave me. My mother drove away whacking me. She turned onto Porter Street and I yelled at her, "Stop hitting me," as I pushed her arm away from me.

She kept yelling, "You've been nothing but trouble since you were born," "You've got a big mouth," my mother continued as she drove with one hand and tried whacking me with her other hand. All I could do was dodge her whacks, yell back at her and question her over and over again, "Why do you hate me so much?" She never answered me. All I did was get dropped off at what I thought was my home by my mother's cousin, but I thought wrong, it obviously wasn't my home.

Finally, we were on Agawam Street where my friend moved and the car went silent as we looked for the house number on the houses we drove by. My mother stopped at 95 Agawam Street and I got out of the car. I walked to the driver's side and took my bag out of the back seat. I shut the door as my mother sped off so fast, I felt the wind of her tires barely missing my foot. I knocked on my friend's new address and she opened the door. "Where's your mother?" she questioned me as I informed her, "She couldn't drive away fast enough." I also told her, "She almost drove my foot over."

My friend's family still had boxes to unpack, pictures to hang and curtains to put up. It was a lot of fun sleeping at Sandi's house the few days I stayed, but I knew school was about to start. I needed school clothes, shoes, a new book bag and so I called my mother. When she answered the phone I told her, "Mom I have to go shopping for school." A few seconds go by and I hear nothing. "Mom are you there?" I said into the phone. "Yes," she responded back. "When are you coming to get me?" I questioned her. My mother answered me, "I'm not." I thought she was kidding. "Mom I want to go home," I continued to tell her. "You know you can't," my mother then proceeded to tell me. I became upset as I questioned her, "Why can't I?" She answered me, "You know why, because of Dave." A part of me hated her for saying that but the other part of me knew it made sense. I hung up the phone while she still talked and I sat outside on my friend's front porch.

Sandi's mother called my mother and then Sandi's mom sat me down. We had a meeting at their dining room table as Sandi's mom whose name was Honoria explained to me how I would be staying with them for a little while. She explained even though she didn't know what went on at my mother's house, she wanted me to know the abuse I suffered there, "Would not happen here," as she continued, "You're safe here." Honoria explained my school and Sandi's school were on the same street. She explained that she and her husband would drive us all to school and pick us up after school every day until we learned to walk without getting lost. Sandi and her older sister were still going to their catholic school on High Street and I would now be going to a junior high school called the Moody school which was also on High Street and just one street over from where my family still lived with Dave on Pleasant Street. Gosh I was a sad kid. Sandi was so cool about it as she gave me hugs and tissues when I needed them. I called my mother the next day, "Mom I still need money for school clothes," I said into the phone. "I'll be right there," my mother snapped before hanging up on me.

She was there a few minutes afterwards, she pulled up to the house and put her hand out her driver's side window. I grabbed the money in her hand and moved myself closer to her so I could talk to her but she sped off without saying a word to me. I watched as she drove away and looked down to see she gave me a lousy thirty dollars to go shopping for school. Honoria took me out shopping and I knew she paid more than the money I was given with all I got for school that day. Sandi also gave me a lot of her hand me down clothes, jackets, winter boots and more. I was already adapted to being in the go play zone, but now I was adapting to the fact my mother chose her boyfriend over her own daughter. I didn't want Sandi to look down on me if she knew what Dave did to me. I didn't want her to look down on me if she knew what I had been through just by the age of eleven years old. I felt so very unwanted by my own family. School started and it went the way I was told it would. Honoria and her husband drove us all to our schools. Dropping me off at my new school where I was starting 7th grade.

I was instantly welcomed by Sandi and her family. I was included in the chores, the rules of the house and never did they make me feel uncomfortable. I was included in trips to their family gatherings. I was included when we were all sent to the neighborhood store for a thirty-cent candy bar. I was included in their daily lives like I was one of their own. At one point Honoria talked to me about nightmares I was having. She let me know I was waking up others by my screams as she explained to me, I was safe in her home. My mother never called me but I did call her many times asking if I could come home and she told me I couldn't come home each and every time. I would cry every time I called her. Sandi and her family always gave me hugs. Honoria and Sandi's older sister would remind me numerous times, "It's not your fault."

*Hearing them say it didn't really help the hurt or shame I was feeling at the time. But as I grew, words of encouragement like those followed and molded me into the person I am today. *

My twelfth birthday was on a school day. No one at school knew it was my birthday and I didn't even realize it was my birthday until I was in school and the date was on the chalkboard in my homeroom. I pretty much kept to myself in school. At recess it was the kids who came in from my old school, kids who came in from the Reilly elementary school and kids who were the veterans of the school, the 8th graders. It was just another normal day for me, Sandi nor anyone in her family knew it was my birthday. We sat down at dinner every night together and talked about a lot of things. I guess we never talked about birthdays and I didn't want to bring it up at dinner that night because I didn't want them to feel bad or look at me with pity. I knew my mother would call me, it was my birthday, of course she's going to call, I told myself about a hundred times as the afternoon went into evening and the evening went into night time. At bedtime I could feel the bucket of tears about to pour down my face as I realized my mother never called. I felt so hurt, mad, empty, family-less and unimportant. 'Why didn't she call?' I questioned myself over and over again. I slept in Sandi's bedroom and we shared a big bed. I cried as quietly as I could without letting her know or keeping her awake. I literally had a huge hole in my heart from the hurt I felt and a huge hole in my stomach from the anger I felt.

I laid in bed that night telling myself I would remember my twelfth birthday for the rest of my life. I didn't get one happy birthday and no cake as no one knew it was my birthday, but my mother did. All I could do was cry myself to sleep. Decorating for the holidays at Sandi's made me want to go home again. I wanted to go home and be with my brothers, my baby sister and my mother. I called my mother and told her when she answered the phone, "Mom I want to come home." She answered, "You know you can't," "You're a troublemaker," she snapped at me. "You're not welcomed here anymore," she said in a cruel manner. I questioned her over and over again, "Why can't I come home?" She answered every time, "You know why, because of Dave." I hated her answers. 'Don't cry,' I told myself as I changed the subject. "You didn't call me on my birthday," I said to my mother, but she said nothing. "I want to come home for Christmas," I then screamed into the phone. "Your friends mother has to give you Christmas now," my mother said insisting it was a normal thing to do. "People do it to troublemakers all the time," she snapped at me. "Is he still there?" I questioned her about Dave and she yelled into the phone, "Jesus Christ of course he is," as she yelled at me to stop asking. "What did you get for your birthday from your friends' family?" she then questioned me in an attempt to change the subject. I replied to her, "Nothing, no one knew it was my birthday." I hung up the phone before I could hear anymore of her toxic voice. Of course, I bawled my eyes out and went into the bathroom to clean my face as I usually did. When I came out of the bathroom Sandi and her mom sat me down to explain how calling my mother only makes me cry. "Maybe it's best if you don't call her for a little while," Honoria said to me and as a freshly new twelve-year-old, I knew she was right.

A Childhood Tragedy Under a Mother's Watch

Christmas was awkward at first, but as the day went on it turned out to be a lot of fun. It didn't even bother me that I didn't wake up to gifts under the tree like I used to because I was just happy to not be abused anymore. Sandi's family made me feel as comfortable as possible. It was my first feel safe Christmas. It made me smile when I reminded myself of it, 'First feel safe Christmas.' All that mattered to me was Dave wasn't getting near me anymore. Soon it was January 1982 and I was being what I was supposed to be, a kid. Hanging out in the neighborhood with Sandi and her sister as we got to know kids in the area. Sandi's backyard had a big slope and we went sledding back there all the time. I didn't call my mother and she didn't call me. One day Sandi's mom told me about picking me up the next day after school. "We will only be a few minutes late," Honoria explained. Informing me I might be the only one left at the school when school got out for the day. "Walk to the corner and wait for us at the crosswalk," she reminded me numerous times and asked me to repeat it back to her. Making sure I wouldn't forget. When school got out, I sat at the stairs as all the kid's left the school. Some kids were walkers, some walked in a single file line to their buses and others ran to awaiting vehicles. Once the school yard became empty, my school looked like a haunted house under the cold winter sky. I decided to walk out of the school yard and over to the corner by the crosswalk.

It was on the corner of High and Rogers Street, directly across from Fort hill park. I stood along the fence outside the school watching as cars drove by. Then there she was, she went flying around the corner as I watched the rear lights of her car. She turned down Sherman Street to go home to Pleasant Street, it was my mother. We made eye contact as she came down Rogers Street, then she gunned her gas pedal as she went around the corner. Then I heard the beep of a car horn and I looked to see Sandi and her family waving at me to get in the car. As we all drove back to Sandi's home, her mom who was in the passenger seat turned to me and said, "Why do you look so sad?" I looked at her and told her, "My mother drove by me right before you came." She then questioned me, "Did she stop?" I shook my head as I told her, "No she didn't stop."

She then said three words to me that would stick with me for decades, "Shame on her," she said. And I thought to myself, 'Yes, shame on her.'

We were all eating dinner one day when the topic of birthdays came up and I was questioned, "When is your birthday, Cathy?" I answered, "December fifteenth," and Sandi's mom was upset I didn't tell them the month before when it was my birthday. She gave me a soft dope slap upside my head and we all laughed. As winter became springtime, the calls to my mother were something I used to do in the past. She never called me and I was having so much fun being a kid living with Sandi and her family that I never called her either. The mayor of Lowell lived across the street and for laughs we would order take-out food to be delivered to their house. We would peak through the windows laughing while one of the older sons would pay for the food even though they didn't order it. We would take a mattress off a bed when the parents weren't home and slide down the inside stairs as we laughed at the fun we were all having. We would watch a new music video every Friday night on MTV music television. Dancing around the house like we owned it. As the school year went on, Sandi and her sister were transferred to St. Peters school on Gorham Street. The three of us started to walk to school. We walked down Agawam Street and down Lawrence Street together then they went their way and I walked straight up Rogers Street to get to my school. I would run as fast as I could across the street when I got to the corner of Pleasant Street, then I continued up to my school. After school I would walk down Rogers Street and meet up with Sandi and her sister, something we continued to do until we got out of school for the summer.

By the summer of 1982, I was doing a lot with Sandi and her family. We went out to play miniature golf, we went to the drive-in, out to eat at restaurants, swimming and more. Then we all went camping, the real way. I slept in a tent with Sandi and not in a camper with a monster. Sandi along with two of her siblings have a dad who lived in another state. They always kept a great relationship even though there was a distance of many states in between them. Once back home from camping, I was told about a trip to their dad's they would be taking in mid-July. "Have you talked to your mother?" Honoria questioned me and I laughed as I told her, "No I haven't." In fact, I had not talked to my mother in many months.

A day or two later Honoria questioned me, "You know your mother moved?" I didn't know she moved and later that day my mother called me to inform me she was coming to get me. "What about him?" I questioned her about Dave. "He's not here," she yelled into the phone before hanging up on me. I packed my bag of clothes I collected while I stayed there and thanked Sandi's mom and stepdad for letting me stay. Sandi and I then went outside to wait for my mother to pick me up. That is exactly what my mother did, she picked me up. She flew up Agawam Street and stopped quickly in front of Sandi's house. I walked to her car, "Don't you want to talk to Sandi's mom?" I questioned my mother. "No, let's go," she snapped at me, "I'm in a rush," she snapped again. I said bye to my friend and we planned to talk after her visit with her dad was over.

My mother said not one word to me as she drove. It was when she turned onto a street, I wasn't familiar with that I questioned her, "Where are we going?" She answered me, "I moved." She then pulled into a small parking lot with a row of apartments. "Where are we?" I questioned her. But she ignored me. After she parked and shut off the car, she pointed her finger in my face, "I wasn't expecting you to come back, go straight up the stairs." my mother ordered me then she said, "I still got to tell Vinny about you." Then she jumped out of her car and ran inside a door along the row of apartments. I got out of the car and headed towards the same door my mother just went in as I said to myself, 'Who's Vinny?' I walked up the two or three steps and opened the door. The number on the door was #33 and the street was Butler Avenue right off of Gorham Street. A part of Lowell which didn't look familiar to me. Once I was inside, I shut the door behind me as I looked throughout the living room to my left and a set of stairs straight ahead from where I was standing. I headed up the stairs to where the bedrooms were.

When my mother dropped me off at Sandi's home on Agawam Street ten months earlier, they still had a lot of boxes to unpack, pictures to hang up and it seemed like they had just moved in, because they did just move in. Being inside Butler Avenue I knew within minutes they have been living there for a while already. Pictures of my brothers and baby sister were on the upstairs hallway walls. There were no boxes full, emptied or folded. I walked upstairs eager to see my siblings. I walked to the doorway of the first bedroom and there was a man I never saw before inside. I quickly walked away to the next bedroom and it was my baby sister's bedroom which was too small to share with me. I walked straight ahead to the third bedroom and it was my older brother's bedroom. I said hello to him and he said hi back. We talked for a few but I wanted to know where my bedroom was so I headed back to the hallway where the stairs were. I walked straight down the hallway and there was a bedroom to my right but it was my mother's bedroom. Hiding in the corner was a door going up to the attic so I went up. The room was filled with unpacked boxes, weights and other things which made me realize I was probably in my oldest brother's bedroom. I headed back down the stairs to the floor with all the bedrooms on it. My mother came up the stairs and I immediately questioned her, "Where's my bedroom?"

She looked at me as if I asked her a confusing question. "What do you mean your bedroom?" my mother questioned in a sarcastic tone. "I didn't know you were coming back," she continued as she walked in circles in the hallway. "Coming back," I said loudly to my mother, "I never left," I continued, "You left me at other people's houses," I reminded her. My mother acted as if it was my fault, I was returned to her while she continued to snap at me, "Well I thought you were living at Sandi's house." I quickly snapped back at her, "I'm your daughter not theirs." But my mother didn't listen to a word I said as she was mad because it was an inconvenience, I was returned to her. She gave me a wobbly cot and had me rest it in the breezeway of the upstairs hallway in between my brother and baby sister's bedroom. She gave me a sheet, told me to use one end of the cot for my clothes and then I questioned her for a pillow. I had no bedroom, no privacy and no bureau for my clothes. Just a cot which I used as my bedroom, bureau and bed. And there I was, home. I walked downstairs and met the guy Vinny. Guess he was my mother's new boyfriend. The guy in the bedroom upstairs was his brother, Jimmy.

I questioned my mother about why my oldest brother's room in the attic wasn't unpacked yet and she informed me, "He's still living on Pleasant Street," "He's finishing his school year there," my mother continued as she told me he would be returning in a couple of days. "That's his bedroom upstairs," she snapped at me. "So don't get any funny ideas," she continued. "Wanting my own bedroom, what a funny idea," I said to my mother as I turned around and headed upstairs to hang in my bed, bureau bedroom. I fell asleep that night thinking to myself, 'I hate my life.' I did, I hated my life.

The next morning, I took clothes downstairs with me and changed in the bathroom. I went back upstairs looking for my mother and I found her folding laundry in her bedroom. After watching her fold laundry for a few minutes, I finally asked her the question I was afraid to ask. "What happened to Dave?" I questioned her. "What do you think happened to him?" she said rolling her eyes at me and keeping her motto of being famous for answering my questions with a question. With a twelve-year-old smart-ass attitude I snapped back at my mother, "I don't know what happened to him," "I wasn't around remember?" I continued as I looked at her waiting for her next response. "Don't be fresh," my mother snapped at me. I continued watching her fold her laundry until she finally answered me. "He went away to jail," my mother said and I jumped up in excitement. "For what he did to me?" I questioned her, "You told the cops?" I questioned as I jumped in excitement. My mother with an ear-to-ear smile, looked at me and said, "Of course I did." I questioned if he could get out of jail but my mother assured me, he was gone for a long time, "At a jail for child pigs," she said. After the excitement of knowing he went to jail for what he did to me, I then wanted to know where my stuff from Pleasant Street was. I asked the question, "Mom where's all my stuff from Pleasant Street?" But she said nothing. My mother ignored me and went back to folding her laundry. I questioned her again, "Mom where's my stuff from Pleasant Street?" Still not a word from her. So, I continued, "Where's the sweater my dad gave me?" "Where's my diary?" "Where's my books?" "Where are all the new clothes you gave me and I could have used last summer?" I continued questioning my mother.

I got tired of her ignoring me and I yelled at her, "Where's my stuff mom?" My mother stopped folding her laundry and told me she couldn't take everything in the move. "Cathy, I had to move this all by myself," she said as she waved her hands throughout her bedroom. "You think Dave helped me?" my mother questioned me. I answered her, "Well I would have helped if I knew." My mother continued talking, "I had to fight him just to clean up that cellar," my mother said as my eyes widened and my stomach felt punched in as I said to my mother, "Mom he was going to put me in there." My mother snapped at me, "You don't know that and don't go around saying that." I was mad she said that to me and I snapped back at her, "Yes I do know for a fact," and then I continued, "Don't worry I don't go walking around telling people I had my mother's boyfriends dick in my," I was cut off as my mother smacked me across the face with her open hand. "Don't be fresh," she snapped at me. The smack hurt but it didn't make me cry. The room went quiet as I watched my mother sorting her folded laundry and putting it away in the bureau drawers. "I'm sorry mom," I said to her as I apologized for the way I spoke.

Then I had another question for my mother. "Did you find those photos?" I questioned her as a pit of vomit rested in my stomach. Nothing could prepare me for my mother's answer to that question as she knew exactly what photos I was referring to, all the camera photos, polaroid photos and film Dave took of me for all those years. My mother answered my question, "Yes I had to give him stuff to put in with the rocks." I looked at my mother in total horror at what she said to me but she quickly started to explain how angry he was with her for keeping me away. She told me he fought with her the whole summer to go get me. "But I knew you were safe at my cousin's," my mother said in an attempt to look as much of a victim to Dave's abuse. "I had to give him some of your stuff," she said. "Those photos and that freaking virgin Mary sex toy just to shut him up," my mother continued as I stood there in total shock, horror and disbelief. My mother informed me, "Look it wasn't easy for me either," as she leaned closer towards me, "And don't go telling what we just talked about to your friends," she continued. I was left speechless. "Hey I had to defend myself from him to you know," she said. Then my mother finally stopped talking. It took a few minutes to sink in all my mother had just said to me. "So those nude photos and films of me are in that cellar wall?" I questioned my mother as I was now tasting the vomit resting in the pit of my stomach. She answered my question, "No one will ever find them as long as you don't go blabbing to anyone," "It's buried good," she continued to say to me. I looked at her in disgust. "Like my body would have been if I didn't run to Sandi's house," I said as I ran out of her bedroom before I could hear her reaction to what I had just said.

I started to explore the neighborhood of what was now my new home. At home I rarely saw my brothers. My oldest brother came home about a week after I got there. My baby sister had friends in the neighborhood already and us being over six years apart, made me too old to hang out with her and her friends. I avoided my mother's new boyfriend Vinny as much as I could. He was cool about it, he didn't make fun of me because of it and he even gave me the space I needed as I adjusted myself to my new home. I would wake up and bring my clothes downstairs with me so I could change for the day in the bathroom.

I would eat a quick breakfast and inform my mother I was going out. "I'm going outside now," I'd say to my mother as she continued doing whatever she was doing at the time and never acknowledging me. I started to wander out of the parking lot I had as a yard. Walking around Butler Avenue and the busy Crosby, Gorham and Chambers Streets of Lowell.

I came to a stream of water known as River Meadow Brook. I would walk along the path of the water and I started spending my mornings and days there. I would walk along the stream until I got to the Lawrence Street mills then I'd turn around and either head back the same way or if the water was low, I would hop across using rocks in the stream of water as stepping stones. Being down by the water I'd take a notebook and pencil with me so I could draw or write if I wanted to.

Sometimes I would get yelled at by an adult to get away from the water. They would watch me as I headed back up to the sidewalk. Once they were out of sight, I headed back down to the stream of water. When that got boring, I started to walk more around the area, walking through the Portuguese neighborhoods and coming out to the busy Lawrence Street. I knew the area from walking to school when I lived at Sandi's house so I kept walking until I got to a small bridge on Rogers Street and looked for ways to get down to that river bank. It was the Concord River and I found a way to its bank by walking to Perry Street and going behind the dog food factory. I would walk along the river and come out onto Church Street. Next time I would walk further the other way and come out on the other end of Lawrence Street by the Lowell cemetery. I got my privacy from those walks. The 1982 riverbanks in Lowell, Massachusetts were nothing like they are now. There were no pop-up tents filled with homeless families, there were no large amounts of litter overflowing the waters and its surrounding grounds. There were no hypodermic needles filling the grounds of our city. The 1982 riverbanks in Lowell were pure serenity for me. It was a calm feeling as I would stare at water flowing over a rock for hours. Reminding myself over and over again, 'It wasn't your fault,' 'I did nothing wrong,' as I'd try not to cry over the horrifying memories going through my head. Continuously reminding myself of the peace and beauty as I explored all nature had to offer me.

After weeks of being back home with my family, I woke one morning and went looking for my mother. I realized her car was gone which meant she was also gone. No one knew where she went as she had left before we all woke up. I didn't leave to go hang outside by the water because I wasn't able to tell her I was going. Even though she never cared when I told her, for some reason I always let her know when I was going outside. I stayed around the house waiting for my mother to return. I sat at the kitchen table, a chair in the living room and up to my bed, bureau and bedroom to sit on my wobbly cot. I heard my mother come in the front door when she slammed it in her rush to get inside. I heard her yelling downstairs, "Who made this mess?" I knew it wasn't me so I stayed upstairs and my mother just as quickly came running up the stairs. I jumped from my wobbly cot and away from my bed, bureau bedroom. I met my mother as she got to the top of the stairs and I was about to tell her I was going outside when she grabbed me by my arm and said, "Get over here," while she shoved me towards her bedroom. I turned around to face her but she shoved me again so I was now in her bedroom.

"What the heck mom," I snapped at her as she grabbed me by my cheeks, squeezing so hard her fingers slipped causing some to go into my mouth. "You keep your freaking mouth shut," my mother pointed her finger into my face as she held me with her other hand by my shirt. "What are you talking about?" I questioned her. "Your sisters freaking father," my mother answered me as she walked in circles inside her room and what seemed to be her head also. "That stupid freaking cellar," my mother said with tears in her eyes. "He took all the freaking rocks out," my mother continued as she looked so stressed. "I thought he was in jail?" I questioned her. She looked at me, "Yes, they let him out to get his stuff," she quickly answered. "I had to give the landlord back the keys," she continued. "The rocks are back," she assured herself as she stepped closer to me pointing her finger in my face, "Don't go blabbing about any of this," "You hear me?" she continued. I just looked at her strangely until finally asking, "Can I go outside now?" "Be back for dinner," she told me. Then she became motherly as she smiled and said, "It will be our secret, ok?" she said as she smiled. I just looked at her like she was crazy. We walked out of her bedroom where I continued to adjust to what was my life.

I had absolutely no privacy in that home. My mother and Vinny would go out weekly to the bar located on the corner of Gorham and Central Street. They were able to take a short cut through our parking lot as the fence was broken down to make for an easy shortcut. My mother left the phone number to the bar and I guess it was something they had been doing for a while before I got unexpectedly returned. Sometimes my mother and Vinny would have friends over for an afternoon or night of card playing. They would let us kid's play with them for a while and pay us a quarter for every beer we retrieved from the refrigerator when requested. I had a fun

1975-1982 Lowell Massachusetts

time one day while playing cards with them and I think that was the first time I realized my mother was jealous of me. She kicked me a few times under the table, gave dirty looks and repeated numerous times, "It's almost bedtime." But it was the next morning when I got a blunt of my mother's jealous streak against me. It was what I did every morning, I woke up and took clothes downstairs so I could change in the bathroom. I was still wearing my hand me down clothes from my mother's cousin's home and clothes from my friend Sandi. Only problem was, I was growing but the clothes weren't. I didn't have much to choose from so I grabbed a pair of shorts and a tank top. I got dressed, went upstairs to put my sneakers on and headed back downstairs.

My mother was setting up to iron some clothes as she opened the ironing board up in the kitchen. It took up a good amount of room in the already squished kitchen with appliances and busy people moving about. I squeezed between the kitchen cabinet and the ironing board as I tried to get into the bathroom. "What the heck are you wearing?" my mother screamed at the top of her lungs. She just as quickly came around the ironing board as she moved it away and began whacking me from behind. I tried to turn to face her but she kept whacking me as I sat myself onto the bathroom floor and rolled myself into a ball until she was done. My older brother, (the same one who said, "You better call mom," in the attic of 1981 Pleasant Street) questioned if I was ok but I just screamed at them all, "Leave me alone."

My head hurt, my arms hurt and I was bawling my eyes out. My mother yelled for me to get out of the bathroom. "Other people have to use it too you know," she snapped. I was breathing heavy as I walked out of the bathroom. "You look like you want attention," my mother snapped at me. "Look how tight your shorts are," she continued with a disgusted look on her face. "Mom these are my only clothes," I said to her in an attempt to defend myself. But then my mother continued in her nasty manner as she questioned me, "What did you pose for those photos too?"

I gasped a breath as I looked at my mother and my eyes swelled up in tears by the buckets. I ran upstairs to bawl my eyes out on my cot. My older brother would walk by and with my baby sister in her room, it meant there was no privacy for me. I needed tissues anyways so I headed back downstairs. I went into the kitchen where my mother was still ironing clothes and I questioned her, "Why are you so mean to me?" But she only answered by yelling at me about how tight my clothes were. "You look like a prostitute," she snapped at me. With tears pouring down my face I said, "I'm your daughter." "You have to buy me clothes," I then yelled at her. She answered by yelling more about my clothes being too tight and I should be wearing bigger clothes. So, I yelled again, "You're my mother, you have to buy me some." She went on complaining, "Where am I going to get money for that?" "Who do you think pays the bills?" she yelled. "Your brothers pay for their own clothes," "Get a job," she finally declared. I looked at her strangely when she told me I had to get a job. "Ummmmm I can't get a job, I'm only twelve years old," I sarcastically snapped at her. "No, you're not," said my mother, "You're thirteen," she continued. "Oh my God mom," I yelled at her, "I'm twelve, do the math," I yelled as I shook my head at her. "Well, you'll be thirteen this year," she said to me before telling me to go upstairs and put on a long t-shirt. That was the end of my mother/daughter talk for that day.

My mother and Vinny continued going over to the bar at the corner and it wasn't long before my mother found me a job. "I got you a job," my mother told me. "Well, if she wants you," she continued as she was always quick to take a jab at my pride. The bartender at the bar my mother and Vinny went to needed a babysitter. The bar was on the first floor of a huge apartment building and she lived in one of the apartments with her daughter. She needed a weekend babysitter and was meeting girls to take the position. I hit it off with her daughter right away and I was hired on the spot. The bartender whose name was Bonnie was in her late twenties and very hip. Her daughter was five years old and her name was Brandy. It started as weekend babysitting only but quickly became weekdays also. Her daughter was always asking for me and soon I was doing sleepovers. Bonnie always had the best snacks, VHS tapes and music for me. I got paid extra if I cleaned the apartment or did the dishes.

If she had a good night and good tips then she paid me extra. Every dollar I made from babysitting went straight to my mother. The agreement was my mother was going to save all my money for the whole month of August and then she would take me out school shopping. I used the shortcut through the broken fence to get back and forth to Bonnie's. Within a couple weeks I was sleeping over even when I wasn't babysitting. Bonnie was so cool; she would blare music and dance throughout her apartment as her daughter and I would join in. Of course, it wasn't long before my mother started to complain about me always being there. "What do you do over there?" she would question me and I would be a smart ass as I reminded her, "Remember that job you had for me?" Before my mother could answer I would say, "There," as I walked away and did my best to avoid my mother when I was home.

One weekday in late August I went to Bonnie's to babysit in the afternoon. I was to be home from babysitting by ten o'clock that night. I was comfortable around Bonnie and she always made me feel as if I was just as important as anyone else in the world. Bonnie was home on time and in a super good mood. She wanted to go back out and I didn't want to go home to sleep on my cot. Bonnie had a king size waterbed I crashed in when I slept over. Some mornings I crawled out of that bed never seeing her in it. To a twelve-year-old it was a huge bed. My mother called a couple of times that night until around eleven o'clock when I finally told her, "I'm sleeping here," as I explained I was alone with a five-year-old. My mother was mad at me but there was nothing she could do. Minutes later Bonnie came back home and cancelled her late night out. We started talking and laughing. She made us hot tea and we talked more. She was so real, she stuck up for herself, had a nice place, a cute kid and she was a super cool person. We played music, talked and laughed until the wee hours of the morning. "Holy crap," Bonnie yelled, "It's four in the morning," she said in surprise as we both looked at the clock. We were totally shocked of how we talked, laughed, ate snacks and drank tea the whole night through as the sun started to shine through the windows.

"Hey can I say something without offending you?" Bonnie questioned me. I shrugged my shoulders and told her yes. She explained how she works the bar sometimes when my mother and Vinny are there. "I only know your mother from the bar but your mother doesn't seem much of a loving mother," Bonnie said to me. I guess I felt comfortable enough with Bonnie to say, "Letting your boyfriend rape your daughter for over six years," as Bonnie just looked at me, "No that doesn't make you a loving mother at all," I continued. Bonnie's eyes swelled up in tears as she hugged me. "I knew I didn't like her," Bonnie said as she expressed her empathy towards my older sister. "Wherever she is," Bonnie said to me with a look of sadness on her face. "No, me," I said to Bonnie. Her reaction of horror just made me bawl my eyes out into her arms. She brushed my hair, rolled a marijuana joint and said, "I probably shouldn't be doing this," before letting me take a few drags from her rolled joint. I stayed a few more hours, showered there and put my clothes back on. Bonnie made sure I didn't look like I cried the Mississippi river before sending me home.

I knew walking home that morning I was in trouble for babysitting overnight. I got home to my mother yelling at me for disobeying her orders. She whacked me twice along my arm as I moved away from her while she yelled, "You're grounded." I took the liberty to question her, "Am I grounded to my room?" Knowing I didn't have a room. My mother told me not to be fresh and informed me I could only babysit for Bonnie on weekends now. "Schools about to start," she reminded me. I then questioned her if we could go school shopping but she informed me she had to go switch my school. She told me I wouldn't be going to the Moody school anymore because the Butler school was just up the street on Gorham Street. "We'll go shopping this weekend," my mother snapped at me.

A day or two later I woke up and my mother was already gone. I assumed she was at the place where she had to go in order to switch my school. She was gone all morning and got home after lunch time. She came in the door complaining about wasting her whole day on, "Changing your school," she said as she looked at me with a disgusted look on her face. Letting me know the inconvenience I was to her. After being in the home for only a few minutes, she headed back out the door, went to her car and came back in the house with a white loud crunching sound bag. "Here," she said to me as she handed me the bag. I looked in the bag and it had sneakers, clothes, a package of underwear, a backpack and pencils. "You went without me?" I questioned her but she just complained about her wasted day on switching my school. I took my new bag of stuff up to my cot and dumped everything from the bag onto it. I grabbed the clothes and headed downstairs to the bathroom so I could try them all on. "Mom," I screamed, "They are high-water," I said to her as I stood before her with my new, too short for me pants. My mother responded, "To bad," and walked away. I was mad, I was not starting 8th grade in high-water pants. I got two new pairs of high-water pants and two shirts which did fit me, a pair of extremely cheap sneakers and an even cheaper backpack.

I gave my mother back the pants telling her, "No way you spent all my money." She insisted she did and how she was too busy to return my pants. "Where did you get them?" I questioned her. "I'll walk there," I continued. But all that did was cause my mother to yell, bitch and complain more. The weekend came and instead of school shopping, my mother insisted all her kids behave because Vinny was taking us all to a carnival. It was a long ride. I think my brothers only went because Vinny wanted them to and not because our mother wanted them to. We got there and we all walked around the place. Vinny offered to pay for everything, games, drinks and carnival snacks. My mother continued to question me over and over again, "Do you want something?" "How about a candy apple?" "Don't you want a prize?" "Some popcorn?" Until she pulled me to the side, "You know your being disrespectful," she whispered into my face. "How?" I looked at her strangely as I questioned her. "He's being nice, buying for everybody and you're being the selfish one by not getting or doing anything," my mother said to me letting me know she was disappointed in me again.

I stood there thinking to myself, 'My mother is whacked.' Then to make peace I said, "Whatever, I'll take a cotton candy." We walked around a little more. I finished my cotton candy and walked over to the trash can to discard it. Everyone kept walking ahead or so I thought. I turned around from discarding my trash and Vinny was waiting on me. We walked alongside each other as we caught up to my mother, brothers and baby sister. When Vinny, keeping his distance said some things I would remember for the rest of my life. Vinny asked to talk with me as he walked along the side of me, "No daughter should be afraid of their mother as you are of her," he said as he pointed his finger to my mother walking ahead of us. He then calmly grabbed my wrist as I slowed down to look at him. "Look honey, I don't know your story but you're a good kid," he continued to say with a smile on his face and I smiled back.

He then bent to my height and said, "Just keep being you ok?" I shook my head to approve his ok as we headed up to where my mother was yelling, "What are you two talking about?" "What were you two talking about?" my mother questioned again. I wasn't sure who she questioned me or Vinny but I said, "Nothing." My mother couldn't let it go. She would tap me on my shoulders or elbow trying to get my attention. "What did you two talk about?" she questioned me as I kept telling her, "Nothing," "Ask Vinny," or "Wouldn't you like to know." I started to dodge her questions as we walked around the carnival. We stopped again for games and drinks as my mother walked over to me again like she was trying to be a friend. Standing next to me, bumping into me as she swayed back and forth. "What did you two talk about?" my mother questioned again in a whispered voice. This time she added, "Don't be fresh either." So, I questioned my mother, "Do you really want to know what he said to me?" A big smile went on her face as she pulled closer to me so she could hear me nice and clear. "No come here," I said to my mother as I moved further away from all the people around us. My mother had an ear-to-ear smile and was eager to hear what Vinny and I had talked about. "Ok you want to know right?" I questioned her again as her head shook up and down. "Hurry," she said to me. "He just told me he wouldn't rape me like Dave did," I said to her as I bolted away from her when the smile dropped from her face. Her smile was dropped quicker than the speed of electricity. I booked it just as quickly and stuck with the others while my mother shot me dirty looks for the remaining day and the whole ride home.

I spent the next few days getting dirty looks and dodging questions because I wouldn't tell my mother what me and Vinny talked about at the carnival. Then later in the week my mother and Vinny headed to the corner bar for their weekly night out. They walked over the same as any other time since I lived there, telling us kids to behave and call the bar if needed. I sat out front for a bit, watched television for a bit and I went to bed on my cot. I was sound asleep when I was woken up by a couple of adults. They were rushing me, "Shhhhh, where are your clothes?" I was questioned in a whispered voice. It was Vinny's brother, a lady and another man. They were surrounding me as they stood over me.

There were all kinds of screaming downstairs. The adults were grabbing clothes off my cot and stuffing them in my arms as they escorted me towards the stairs. Vinny's brother blocked me as we made it down the stairs. I was able to see what all the yelling was, it was my mother. She was being held back by a few people because she wanted to stab me to death. I saw the big knife in her hand as Vinny was pushing her away from getting to me. There was so much commotion as I was rushed out my front door with Vinny's brother, a big pile of clothes in my arms, a blanket over me and a slam of my front door. I was thrown out of my own home again. I was in the parking lot, it was really dark out, a lot of screaming as Vinny's brother wrapped the blanket around me. "Come on," he said to me as he escorted me to the apartment right next door to where my family lived. He told me to lay on the couch and go back to sleep. I was given a pillow and pretended to fall asleep while trying to listen to everything Vinny's brother and the people who lived in the apartment were talking about. Then Vinny's brother left and the lights went out after another blanket was laid on me. I cried and fell asleep.

I awoke the next morning and she was a super nice lady who lived there. She had a lot of kids and her youngest was older than me. Some were moved out already or away a lot. "Call me Mrs. Landry." she said. "And my husband is Mr. Landry," she continued. She got me some cereal then told me how her and her husband had not been out in decades until last night. They decided to take a walk to the corner bar. "Good Lord, I'd hate to know what would have happened if we weren't there," she said to me with a smile.

I questioned the nice lady before me, "Why am I here?" She explained, "There's no excuse for how your mother acted," "Just stay here until she cools down," she said to me. I was still confused, "But why am I here?" I questioned her again. "I guess you said something you shouldn't have said to the bartender," Mrs. Landry said to me. "Just let your mother cool off," she continued. I knew right away Bonnie must have confronted my mother at the bar about what I told Bonnie about myself. Mrs. Landry then took me around the apartment. It was set up the same as next door except the parents had the smallest room. Two bedrooms were split apart by a breezeway, one side for girls and one side for boys. I didn't have to sleep on a cot in the breezeway, I got a bed on the girl's side. I was told the house rules were to clean up after yourself, be on time for meals and for me to just be a kid. She served meals on the big kitchen table they had. At breakfast there would be boxes of cereal on the table lined with a gallon of milk, bowls and spoons.

I sat quietly on their couch, ate when I was supposed to and went to bed when I was told for days while my family lived right next door. Mrs. Landry told me about school starting and questioned if I had school supplies. I told her my mother got me some. I asked if I could go next door to get my stuff for school and she agreed it was ok to do so. I headed next door to where my family lived, I went to open the door but it was locked. I knocked on it but no one answered. My mother's car was outside, so I knocked again.

The door opened a little and I was about to go inside when I was blocked. My mother snapped at me, "You're dead to me," and slammed the front door shut. I stood there for a few moments deciding, 'Do I cry?' or, 'Do I knock again?' I knocked again, she opened it and I yelled, "I need my school stuff." My mother rolled her eyes as she said, "Wait a minute," and shut the door again. Returning moments later as she opened the door and threw a bunch of clothes, notebooks and pencils at me while yelling at me to never knock on her door again. Some stuff I caught and other stuff fell all over the steps and ground. I picked up everything and headed back over to the Landry home where I cried and tried to figure my life out as I was about to start 8th grade at a new school. I couldn't understand why my mother hated me so much. I was so heartbroken over her telling me I was dead to her. Mrs. Landry was upset also. She was about to go over and give my mother a piece of her mind. She wanted to know what my mother said to me and when I told her she said I was dead to her, Mrs. Landry got very upset. She then questioned me, "What did you say to that bartender?" I froze at her question at first and then answered her," I babysat for her last month and I told her my mother isn't a good mother to me." I knew for a fact Bonnie confronted my mother, a part of me smiled inside at the thought Bonnie had stuck up for me.

But I was just a sad kid, not only over the childhood my mother gave me, what my mother did to me since I ran to my friend's house a year earlier or what my mother has done to me since I was returned just two months earlier. No, I was a sad, hurt, unwanted, family-less twelve year old kid because of what my mother did to me my whole young life. Even with all the years of horrific abuse I suffered, I was still just a kid who wanted her family. I was afraid to go outside when I lived at the Landry home, I was afraid of my mother. I was shy being inside the Landry home because I didn't really know anyone. Their youngest daughter Darlene took me for a walk to the Butler school so I knew how to get there. It was literally a five-minute walk from Butler Avenue. Darlene was funny and, on our way, walking she said to me, "Hey sorry your mother's a douche," and then she says, "That sucks huh?" She stopped walking to give me a hug. I was laughing at her calling my mother a douche and walking to the school was going to be an easy walk. We headed back to her home where I showered as school was starting the next day.

I woke up with a pit in my stomach. Mrs. Landry made me toast as all I saw was sadness and pity in her eyes. I could tell she felt bad for me. She made me lunch with snacks and a drink. I started school wearing high-water pants, no haircut and no family. I left for school by walking straight across the Butler Avenue parking lot so I wouldn't have to walk by my mother's door and I walked back from school the same way. I stayed as far away from the front door of my family's apartment as I could. I was in 8th grade at a new school, living with strangers right next door to my family. Mrs. Landry had bags of old clothes and went through them while I was in school. I got pants, sweaters, a fall jacket and she washed them all for me. She wanted my new school pants my mother got me so she could add a hem to them. Then she handed me a bag with a box in it. She bought me a pair of better-looking shoes, they were black work boots and I loved them. A few days later her relative came over and cut my hair for me.

The Landry's also bought an Atari gaming system along with a game called pacman. There were rules set on when to play. I did my homework and stayed in as much as I could. I met the Landry's nephew who stopped over all the time because he went to school with his cousin who lived there. It wasn't long until we were having pacman competitions. We'd keep score and continue the next day or weekend. After a couple of days coming over to play, their cousin said to me, "Who the heck are you?" as he laughed. "You're in the same seat every time I come here," "Do you move?" he continued smiling and laughing as he talked. I told him who I was, then he told me his name was Mark Delong and he came over for his aunts cooking all the time. "Why are you living here at my aunts?" he questioned me. "Because my family doesn't want me," I answered him and he responded, "Ouch." I lived with the Landry family for the full month of September. I only left the Landry's home for school unless I went for rides with Mrs. Landry in her car. I never communicated with any of my family members who lived right next door. The Landry's nephew Mark said to me one day, "You need a brother, I'm here." We had a serious game of pacman going on between us. Soon we were in our own competition of who was the better pacman player. We would play in the living room of the Landry's home for hours.

One day in early October Mark showed up at the Landry home. I was playing Atari when Mark says to me, "Hey I think I go to school with your brother, maybe?" I questioned what his name was and when he answered me, "Roland." I said to him, "Yup he lives next door." Mark looked at me strangely and said, "What?" "Next door there?" he questioned me as he pointed his finger to the wall. I answered him, "Yes." Mark shook his head, stood up, walked over to the wall and said, "Here?" as he tapped on the wall. I laughed at him as I answered, "Yes." Mark sat down on the couch. It was Mark's turn on pacman and pacman died instantly. Everyone in the room looked at Mark and he was still in the same position when he sat down with a confused look to his face. He was baffled as to why my family lived next door and I was living with his aunt and uncle. He questioned me, "Why?" I answered his question with a question, "What, why my family lives next door and I'm living here with your family?" He answered immediately, "Ya." I responded, "Yes, that I don't know." Mark couldn't understand why my family lived next door and he wanted to know why. "Want to go ask my mother with me?" I questioned him. Mark jumped up and said, "Yup." We headed out the door and over to the Landry's neighbors, my family. I knocked on the door and my mother answered but she shut the door as soon as she saw it was me. So, I knocked again. She flung the door open, "What do you want," she snapped at me. I immediately questioned her, "Why am I living next door?" She noticed Mark standing next to me as we waited for her to answer. She looked back at me and said, "Call Sandi and see if you can stay with her." The door then slammed shut. I looked at Mark who stood there saying, "That did just happen." "That did just happen," Mark continued to say as we walked back to the Landry home. He was shocked a mother could be so cruel to her own daughter.

Mrs. Landry got Sandi's phone number from the telephone book and I called her. We arranged for her mom and stepdad to pick me up for a weekend sleepover on Columbus Day weekend. Mrs. Landry gave me a duffle bag for my clothes and told me, "Take all your clothes." I didn't have to worry about going back for my clothes if I didn't have to. I didn't have much for clothes but I had more than I had in recent years. I thanked Mr. and Mrs. Landry for being so nice to me. I walked out the door and away from my family's front door. I walked across the parking lot and onto the sidewalk as I waited for Sandi and her parents to pick me up.

A Childhood Tragedy Under a Mother's Watch

While I waited on the sidewalk, I turned to look at the front door of 33 Butler Avenue and thought of the people who were inside, they were my family and I was so unwanted by them. But why? They all knew I was next door living with the Landry family. They all knew I suffered severe beatings on Pleasant Street. They all knew they failed to call the police on my abuser. I was twelve years old standing on a sidewalk with a duffle bag of clothes feeling an empty gut wrenching, heart tearing, unwanted hurting sadness. My family could never imagine how lonely and unwanted I felt that day and I would one day grow up to realize they didn't care either.

I had to fight to not be abused anymore, a fight that made me lose out on my family, but a fight that made Dave Umpleby never touch me again. That was the moment I knew my childhood tragedy was over and not knowing I would spend the next thirty years debating if it was worth the fight.

Four
From The Author

CHILD SEXUAL ABUSE IS THE least talk about issue when you are the victim. As a child, you are feared and shamed into silence. As an adult, you are embarrassed and humiliated into silence. When the pity is easier to look at than what the communication will tell, we as children are told to move on and forget. As adults, we are told forgive. Yet, we live our whole lives trying to forget something we will always remember and search for forgiveness in what is so unforgivable. There are statistics all over the world on facts related to child sexual abuse. The truth is, the majority of sexual abused children live their lives never telling their story. Many leave journals behind that only get buried under a heaping pile of family secrets.

I am the little girl in this book, all grown-up and shattering her silence in hopes to bring awareness towards a horrifying crime against children.

A Childhood Tragedy Under a Mother's Watch

What actually happens behind the term 'child molestation?' What does a grown evil demented person do to a child behind a closed door? We only get one life to tell our story and I hope by doing so, I can bring comfort to those who can relate and an understanding to those who don't.

From late 1975 until the last attack on me in 1981, I was abused by a man who continued to rape and terrorize my childhood because he was allowed to by a mother who continued to defend his actions towards her own daughter. From telling my birth mother of a cloth he made me smell on Fletcher Street to a jug of blue liquid she found tucked under her bed on Pleasant Street, Throughout the years of 1975-1981, I went to my birth mother about things her boyfriend was doing to me. I was forced to believe it was normal to have family secrets and to be ashamed of talking about being abused. My abuser's frustrations with me started on Fletcher Street as I would cry and fight him from forcing me to do sexual things. At the time I didn't know what sexual was. I just knew I hated it, he hurt me and I was petrified of him. Though I cried and fought him each and every time, I was just a kid who was overpowered by a man who tossed me as if I was a rag doll.

As my birth mother continued to be caught in lies and realizing she was never going to stop my abuser as she kept telling me she would, I started to question the way of living she allowed me to get used to. My abuser had no intentions of letting me live past my twelfth birthday and I am one hundred percent positive if I did not run to my friend's house that Saturday morning, causing my friend's mother to call my birth mother at her work, my body would someday have been found in that cellar wall. And I am one hundred percent positive my birth mother would have defended him again.

I don't know what happened to the social workers who used to visit, my school, my doctors, my brothers or what family I had, but I was left to deal with what I had been through alone, because my birth mother was mad that I fought to not be abused anymore. I turned to a mother who turned me away, I looked up to brothers who looked the other way and I have a baby sister who would never believe her father was capable of being the monster he was.

Between late summer of 1981 and until my abuser moved out of my childhood home in July of 1982, the city of Lowell and neighboring town of Chelmsford would be subjected to multiple unsolved murders.

My story isn't about a man who may have been nice to some but terrorized my childhood. My story isn't about degrading a woman who gave me birth but failed miserably at being a mother. My story is about me and the so many children who have lived, deal or face a childhood I once lived. My story is about the little girl in photos and film, buried in a cellar wall. My story is about the monster my birth mother harbored.

The traumatizing, horrifying sexual and physical abuse was finally over for me, but the emotional, mental and psychological abuse from my own family was only beginning.

Where was my father? The families who took me in, the truth behind a mother's lies, terrifying repressed memories and a horrifying reality, continues in part two of my memoir: *A Life Given To Me,* Summer of 2022.

Thank You

A home that lacked love, I had nowhere to turn.
That suddenly changed with your cause of concern.
You did not scare me; your approach was kind.
A child afraid to go home didn't sit well in your mind.
That call you made, caused them both to fear
Of what did I say and what did you hear?
During the summer when I wasn't around,
You continued to ask, to them you were a hound.
You are my savior for all that you did.
You saved a child from the acts they hid.
So much abuse, I once had to cope.
Your act of kindness gave me reason to hope.

Dedicated to Honoria... Thank you for saving me.

About the Author

Catherine Mellen is an American poet, author and blogger. Born in 1969 Lowell Massachusetts. She wrote her first poem at age fourteen and quickly adapted her love for words. Shamed by the childhood she lived, she became a cook and caterer for nearly three decades. An auto accident at age forty-five, left her disabled and a victim to horrifying repressed memories. She shares her story of horrific childhood trauma and the courage to shatter her silence on family secrets through her words of poetry and decades of writing in journals.

In 2018 she started a blog where she shattered her silence on childhood trauma, family secrets and unsolved murders in her hometown.

Her poetry has been published in numerous poetry journals and she is the author of Christmas in Poetry Land and Survivor's Mind. Which is the poetry behind her lifetime of living in shame, secrets and silence along with the courage, strength and survival she wrote with each poem.

When Catherine isn't writing, she can be found enjoying her time with her children, granddaughters and friend's.

Read about her life but don't have any pity, she is a strong Irish girl from an all-American city.

www.ingramcontent.com/pod-product-compliance
Lightning Source LLC
LaVergne TN
LVHW041333080426
835512LV00006B/441